City of Men

City of Men

*Masculinities and Everyday
Morality on Public Transport*

ROMIT CHOWDHURY

Rutgers University Press

New Brunswick, Camden, and Newark, New Jersey

London and Oxford

Rutgers University Press is a department of Rutgers, The State University of
New Jersey, one of the leading public research universities in the nation.
By publishing worldwide, it furthers the University's mission of dedication
to excellence in teaching, scholarship, research, and clinical care.

Library of Congress Cataloging-in-Publication Data
Names: Chowdhury, Romit, author.
Title: City of men : masculinities and everyday morality on public transport /
Romit Chowdhury.
Description: New Brunswick, New Jersey : Rutgers University Press, [2023] |
Includes bibliographical references and index.
Identifiers: LCCN 2022052736 | ISBN 9781978829503 (paperback) |
ISBN 9781978829510 (hardback) | ISBN 9781978829527 (epub) |
ISBN 9781978829534 (pdf)
Subjects: LCSH: Transportation—India—Kolkata. | Men—India—Kolkata. |
Urban space—India—Kolkata. | Kolkata (India)—Social conditions—21st century.
Classification: LCC HE311.I4 C47 2023 | DDC 388.40954/147—dc23/eng/20230421
LC record available at https://lccn.loc.gov/2022052736

A British Cataloging-in-Publication record for this book is available
from the British Library.

Illustrations by Subhajit Das

References to internet websites (URLs) were accurate at the time of writing. Neither
the author nor Rutgers University Press is responsible for URLs that may have
expired or changed since the manuscript was prepared.

♾ The paper used in this publication meets the requirements of the American
National Standard for Information Sciences—Permanence of Paper for Printed
Library Materials, ANSI Z39.48-1992.

rutgersuniversitypress.org

For my parents, Susmita Chowdhury and Prithviraj Chowdhury...and for Anima Sarkar

It all means more than I can tell you. So you must not judge
what I know by what I find words for.
—Marilynne Robinson, *Gilead*

Contents

City of Men

Introduction

City of Men

In South Asian urban landscapes, men are everywhere. As you travel through a city in this region, you will inevitably witness groups of men engaged in a range of activities in the outdoors. Let us say that you are in Kolkata, India. In the early morning, walking through one of the few urban parks, you might overhear the sound of laughter, or even raucous disagreement, spilling over from a gathering of elderly men. Perhaps it is midday and you are in an autorickshaw, waiting for the traffic light to turn green. As you look out of the small three-wheeled vehicle that carries as many as five people at a time, you might see men huddled together against the windowpane of an electronics shop, peering at a large television screening a cricket match. The autorickshaw depot, from which you took this popular mode of transport—which has not one woman driver—might have been next to a roadside tea stall. There, you are likely to have seen men sitting around, talking over endless cups of tea, as they often do in these neighborhood tea kiosks. As evening dawns and the working day draws to a close, more join the assembly of men playing cards or a game of carom on street corners. The congregation at the tea stalls adds numbers too.

Or perhaps it is very late at night, and as you step onto the street, you realize that the only transport available to you at that hour is a taxi. The one cab you come across seems to have been deserted by the driver; then you realize that he is sleeping inside the vehicle. You might wonder if these migrant taxi drivers ever feel unsafe, working in the city into the early hours of the day. The bar you just left—not the upmarket pub but one of those that dot the commercial districts of the city, popular among clerks and tradesmen—had but a few women, if any at all. City nights, even more than the day, belong to men.

Indeed, while most men inhabit city streets without either explanation or apology, for women, the right to be in public is hard-won on an everyday basis. And yet we do not seem to know very much about precisely what men do in city spaces as men. What do they talk about? What are the interactional dynamics between different groups of men on city streets? What do they think about the presence of women in public? How do men relate to the urban spaces that they routinely inhabit? What do these modes of relatedness tell us about the gendering of urban spaces in South Asian cities?

This book presents an ethnographic exploration of the linkages between "heterosexual" masculinities and urban spaces. Drawing on insights from the interdisciplinary fields of urban studies, mobility studies, and critical studies of men and masculinities, the project responds to two broad questions. The first, which is an empirical query, asks, in what ways do men inhabit city spaces? The second, which is a theoretical one, asks, how do men's inhabitations of urban spaces produce the city as gendered? The book attends to these concerns by following the laboring lives of two groups of public transport workers—autorickshaw and taxi operators—in contemporary Kolkata and their interactions with traffic police and commuters. Transport labor in Kolkata, and in South Asia more generally, is a thoroughly masculinized industry—it is composed entirely of men and is seen as a job that is proper for men. And it is transportation, more than anything else, that connects every aspect of life in cities, from the residential unit to the neighborhood to the wider urban region (Hanson 1995). Moreover, while women are routinely tied to stasis, mobility is cast as a masculine value (Clarsen 2013). By tracking the geographies of masculinity and public transportation, this book unravels the everyday place-making rituals through which city spaces become gendered. In

India, recurring episodes of gender-based violence in moving vehicles have brought into sharp focus the social relations between working-class male transport workers and the upwardly mobile Indian woman (Amrute 2015). This book brings into view the connections between men's styles of inhabiting urban spaces and the reproduction of gender inequality in cities by foregrounding the micropolitics of copresence on public transportation.

In the dominant public imaginary in Kolkata—and in urban India more generally—motorized forms of public transport and their drivers are the very picture of urban disorder. Both the English language and the so-called vernacular presses portray the autorickshaw and taxi driver as the *lumpenproletariat*, a menacing threat to women's safety and public order in the city. A 2016 *Telegraph* report bearing the headline "Woman 'Captures' Rogue Cabbie" details an incident in which a young middle-class woman working as a bank officer was pushed out of a taxi by the driver for refusing to pay an inflated fare. The woman is reported to have said, "I mostly travel alone and have to tackle such rogue drivers regularly. I know how to deal with them and I think every woman in Calcutta should do so." Another story by the same newspaper, published in 2012, reports the misdemeanor of a taxi driver who allegedly demanded that a woman passenger, whose four-year-old daughter had vomited in the taxi, pay him INR2,000 as compensation. A *Times of India* article from 2016 narrates the plight of a woman filmmaker who found her taxi driver masturbating as the vehicle was stuck in gridlock. Yet it is not just as passengers that women face street harassment from public transport vehicle operators. In 2020, an immigrant taxi driver from a lower caste was promptly arrested for making lewd gestures and comments at a prominent upper-caste Bengali actress and member of Parliament while she was driving her car alongside his taxi.

In public perception, while the entry of mobile-application-based taxi services initially gave hope for middle-class women's safety in the city, the rising incidence of crime perpetrated by Uber and Ola cab drivers has quickly abated such expectations of security. In 2016, a young woman jumped out of a moving Uber after the driver threatened to rape her and dump her body in a ditch. Transport workers' reported misdeeds range from sexual assault to capricious service. Letters written by readers to the editors of prominent English-language dailies convey the great dissatisfaction of the urban middle class toward public transport workers. As one letter puts it, "Stubborn, audacious and outrageous are the words that describe the behaviour of taxi drivers in Calcutta. . . . At night, they are either drunk or desperate to earn the extra buck. The city police are more their accomplices than responsible public servants." Another letter remarks on a driver's improper attire: "The driver was not properly dressed. He was wearing only a vest without sleeves." Not only residents in Kolkata but visitors as well speak of "dodging the shabby rickshaws and careless taxis that pollute the streets" (Christensen 2004, 40).

Indeed, if taxi operators are seen to be wanting in refinement and the police in cahoots with them, autorickshaw drivers make a similar imprint on the urban middle class. It is common to encounter newspaper headlines screaming "auto-cracy," punning on the words "autorickshaw" and "autocracy" to signal the reign of terror apparently orchestrated by auto drivers on the roads of Kolkata. In late 2013, the *Statesman* reported that autorickshaw drivers in a Muslim-majority neighborhood had stopped workers from repairing tram tracks in the locality since the availability of tram services in the area would negatively impact their business. Stories of autorickshaw operators molesting women passengers appear frequently in the news. Even as the media bemoans the powerlessness of the police to handle the "auto menace," autorickshaw drivers themselves routinely protest against police atrocities. In early 2014, the transport minister organized a meeting with the union to discipline autorickshaw drivers with respect to misconduct with passengers, flouting traffic laws, recurring strikes, and overcharging. As a *Times of India* report about autorickshaws in 2018 avers, "Harassment [is] not new for daily commuters." Such indictments of transport workers are to be seen in relation to a more general attitude toward the urban poor in Kolkata and India. In late 1996, for instance, the then-left-front government in West Bengal removed hawkers and informal vendors from the city streets over-night in what was called Operation Sunshine. The initiative was meant to impose middle-class values of order and hygiene in urban spaces and restore the "gentleman's city" (Roy 2004). Such violent state measures to displace the urban poor from their places of work and residence chime with middle-class citizen initiatives in other megacities in India, where aesthetic (Ghertner 2015) and environmental (Baviskar 2002) ideas are deployed to govern urban populations. Postliberalization, a new transnational urban imaginary has emerged in South Asia, wherein images of poverty that have long been emblematic of cities in the region have given way to images of globalized consumer culture (Anjaria and McFarlane 2011).

What do masculinities have to do with such scenarios, and how do they intersect with other social identities in the spaces of everyday urban mobilities? While the families of most autorick-shaw drivers in Kolkata have lived in the city for several genera-tions, most taxi drivers are first-generation migrants, many from the nearby states of Bihar, Chhattisgarh, and Jharkhand. The major-ity of taxi drivers belong to the lower castes and are Hindu, but in some localities of the city most autorickshaw drivers are Muslim. As first-generation single migrants, many young taxi drivers cohabit in shared rooms, while most auto drivers live with their families in urban slums. Since autorickshaws in Kolkata, unlike in other Tier 1 Indian cities, traverse designated routes on a shared basis, their drivers' experience of urban space is patterned differently from that of taxi operators who roam the entirety of the city's landscape. This difference in geography of operation, together with their dif-ferent social identities, influences their relationships with each other, commuters, and traffic police. The ethnography presented in this book unravels the gendered shades of copresence in com-muting spaces and draws thought to the spatial politics that pro-duces different urban worlds for different men in the same city. Sociological investigations of urban interactions, to the extent that these are anchored in conflict theories of society, have considered much less the role of cooperation in holding together the urban social. This book takes cognizance of this tradition in urban studies, while situating itself within those conceptual approaches to urban life that emphasize collaboration between urban actors and the rituals, pleasures, and politics of cooperation (Sennett 2012; Simone 2019). In Kolkata, for instance, regular autorickshaw passengers come to recognize faces of some vehicle drivers in their neighborhoods; for operators too, some passengers become familiar faces. Such neighborly familiarity conditions how gender and everyday cooperation come to matter for urban mobility and city life.

A middle-class woman in her fifties remembers a time some fifteen years ago when she was trying to return home from school with her two young children: Heavy monsoon rain has flooded the streets. There is no transport available. She can't get on the bus because she is carrying too much stuff and two unruly children would be impossible to manage on a crowded bus. As the rainfall intensifies and more time passes without access to any conveyance, her distress grows: How long will they be stranded there? How will she get home? Surely her children will fall sick from being wet and cold. Suddenly she recognizes an autorickshaw driver from her neighborhood. She has traveled on his vehicle several times. Desperate, she hails him, waving her hand in frenzy. The driver recognizes her and slows down in front of her. Even though he is not working at that hour and is on a personal trip, the driver agrees to ferry them home. More than a decade has passed since that inclement day; in this time, one of her children has died. But the woman's voice still registers heartfelt appreciation that the autorickshaw operator drove them right to their doorstep and refused to take the extra money she offered him for his kindness. While conflict and violence take prominence in reports of interactions on public transport, incidents of such generosity abound in commuters' and vehicle operators' narratives of mobility in the city. This book reveals everyday moral expectations from men and women that influence both conflict and cooperative gestures on public transport and what they tell us about patriarchal structures in a changing city.

Rather than being an achievement of democratic entitlements, middle-class women's entry into the public world of commercial work in urban Bengal was compelled by the successive events of the Bengal famine of 1943 and the Partition of Bengal during political independence in 1947 (Bagchi 1990). The figure of the middle-class working woman and men's reactions to her sudden participation in public life, therefore, emerged as key tropes in many prominent Bengali films of the period, of which Ritwik Ghatak's *Meghe Dhaka Tara* (1960; The cloud-capped star) and Satyajit Ray's *Mahanagar* (1963; The big city) are considered classics. Since the 1970s there has been a rise in middle-class women's participation in white-collar employment in Kolkata. In 1970, the female working population in West Bengal represented just 4.43 percent of the total working population. By 1981, the figure had increased to 5.97 percent (Husain and Dutta 2014). Urban women's entry into economic life witnessed a major transformation in the 1990s, following liberalization. The growth of the consumer economy has opened a wide range of job opportunities to both men and women, such as those in marketing and product promotion, health care, banking, hospitality and event management, air travel, and retail. In the software sector of the IT industry, one in every four workers is a woman, whereas in the BPO sector women are twice as numerous as men (Husain and Dutta 2014). Young urban middle-class women's newfound economic self-sufficiency through employment in transnational customer service has unsettled some traditional forms of Indian family life and won them some conditional freedoms (Pal and Buzzanell 2008). The harmful impact of structural adjustment policies on women's lives notwithstanding, research shows that individual women largely feel empowered by their access to new forms of employment (Ganguly-Scrase 2003). A study of young workers in Kolkata's retail industry shows that both single and married women see their jobs as a way of securing autonomy from parental and spousal

control within the family (Gooptu 2009). The circuits of public transport in the city—specifically their gendered patterns—that constitute the mainstay of this project need to be understood in the context of new economies of work and changing spatial structures of present-day Kolkata.

The implementation of the government of India's Mega City Programme in 1996 led to a change in the urban policy of the Kolkata Metropolitan Development Authority (KMDA). From improving the conditions of urban slums, KMDA began focusing on building middle-class housing complexes, glitzy shopping destinations, and new towns on the fringes of the city (Chakravorty 2000; Sen 2017). This form of urban restructuring has fashioned new patterns in the built environment, expressed, for example, in the demolition of old neighborhoods, the destruction of the city's wetlands and their ecology, and the development of the eastern fringes of the city to make way for gated residential communities (Dey, Samaddar, and Sen 2013). In addition to deepening urban inequalities, such patterns of urban development have been attended by transformations in urban culture. The *rowak* (a narrow ledge against middle-class residential houses, around which young men would gather for *adda*—meandering, informal chats among friends) is fast disappearing from the map of Kolkata's landscape. Some commentators (Ray 2012) have claimed, therefore, that these changes in the spatial structure of the city have led to a devaluation of certain cultures of taste and the life of the mind in a city that has been both reviled and revered for these proclivities. The idea of the twenty-four-hour city, though slow to dictate the imagination of urban planners and policy makers in West Bengal, is gradually consolidating itself as nightlife in the city becomes corporatized and private hospitals, upmarket entertainment venues, and round-the-clock services of the global economy widen their ambit in Kolkata. An image of global India has influenced these recent urban transformations, with urban planners and politicians engineering these changes to lure Bengalis living overseas to invest in and return to the city they once called home (Bose 2015). In this climate, if working-class men are being cast as unruly and the principal threat to women's safety and the image of a global city in India, this picture of masculinity is closely related to the ideological promises of urban transformations in the region.

The working-class men who labor as transport vehicle operators in Kolkata are thus part of a changing gender and urban landscape. Historically, the erstwhile left-front government, since coming to power in 1977, had ignored urban development in favor of strengthening its rural vote base. Although Kolkata was British

India's first capital city, through the 1960s until the 1980s Bengal saw capital steadily receding from its folds. By the end of the 1980s, West Bengal ranked eleventh among twenty-five Indian states in terms of state domestic product, and rates of unemployment in the region were among the highest in the country (Roy 2003). The left-front government's attitude to capital and its hostility to economic reform changed in the 1990s. Following the liberalization of the Indian economy, the state government in West Bengal began to engineer urban infrastructure development, in part to cater to the changed value system of the new urban middle classes. Postliberalization, the city's middle classes have increasingly come to identify overpasses, highways, bridges, malls, multiplexes, and gated neighborhoods as indices of a desired urban transformation (Donner 2012). A stream of newspaper articles and television reports drew attention to the abysmal condition of the city's roads, squalor, and unreliable services of urban provisioning. To the new car-owning middle class, overpasses suddenly emerged as architectural icons of convenience and speedy mobility in the city (Donner 2012).

The contestations between 2006 and 2008 around a private company setting up a manufacturing unit in the state for a new "people's car" that was advertised as affordable to "everyone" capture the new political discourses of city development and urban culture in the region. India's new middle classes received news of a car that would cost only INR1,00,000 with much alacrity. As Nielsen (2010, 146) writes, "The low price of Tata's new car meant that many among the middle class could now reasonably aspire for car ownership, the small car also became symbolic of India's rise in the postreform era as a truly competitive, innovative and global economic player in its own right." This meant, however, that in Singur (30 kilometers from Kolkata), where the company was to establish its manufacturing unit, nearly a thousand acres of agricultural land would be converted into an industrial zone, as per the Land Acquisition Act of 1894. While apparently against such practices of accumulation by dispossession, the leader of the opposition party at the time, Mamata Banerjee (the current chief minister of the state), supported the Singur Movement that erupted to arrest this takeover but was at pains to convince the urban middle classes that she was not against industrial development through private capital investment (Nielsen 2010). The urban middle classes' predilection for an affordable private vehicle over farmers' ownership over their land indicates, simultaneously, a collective disregard for the poor's right to livelihood and a desire for a certain kind of city life—free-wheeling mobility in a private bubble, unencumbered by contact with the urban poor. Passengers will relish the risky maneuverings of the autorickshaw as it moves through the crevices of traffic because it facilitates their movement but are annoyed by the same while traveling in their private cars. The desire here is also for a mode of urban mobility that is free of contact with what the urban elite considers corrupt and unruly.

In rural Bihar, where a significant number of taxi drivers in Kolkata are from, almost every household depends on income generated by male family members' labor in cities. Due to the lack of land reforms in Bihar, agriculture in the state did not lead to modern industries (Kumar 2009). Farm work in Bihar is often seen as a paradox: ensuring food against market fluctuations even as it is inadequate for supporting household expenses. Through the course of their lives, a vast percentage of men in rural Bihar oscillate between the village and the city to earn their livelihood (Kantor 2020). Transformations in agrarian relations in the region, from the 1960s, ushered in attendant changes in both the iconography and self-understanding of the farmer; from being a valued symbol of the nation, the farmer began to connote a life of deprivation (Kantor 2020). The migration of men from rural Bihar to Kolkata has been circular, wherein they continue to maintain close links to their village communities. As de Haan (2002) notes, this circulatory pattern of migration in the region has persisted for well over a hundred years, even though relatively permanent employment opportunities have been available in the city. For the Indian urban elite, the migrant Bihari male is a metaphor for an undesired past that it assumes to have transcended (Kumar 2009). The tremendous loathing directed at Bihari taxi drivers comes from an intense desire to be at many removes from a culture that is ethnically stereotyped as backward, boorish, and likely criminal. Middle-class pedagogy about transport workers, especially taxi drivers, instills an anxiety about being taken for a ride. Young people who are beginning to travel alone in the city will be cautioned by older kin about being overcharged and the tricks taxi drivers allegedly deploy to cheat credulous passengers. For the middle-class commuter, being alert to transport workers' supposed trickery is established as a valuable skill of city living. To travel by public transport, as we will see in the chapters that follow, is to confront various moral dispositions and aesthetic judgments in the city, which are implicitly marked by norms of masculinity.

Attempts to revitalize the ailing economy of West Bengal have not hindered a vast flight of human capital from Kolkata. From 2001 to 2011, the city witnessed around 76,000 people leaving the city; during this time, its growth rate was −1.67 percent (Shaw 2015). Moreover, the rise of census towns (smaller urban centers categorized as such by the census in India) in West Bengal between 2001 and 2011 created new venues for employment in the region for migrants from near and afar, besides Kolkata. Demographic shifts are also discernible within different areas of the city. In central Kolkata, which has some of the oldest wards of the city, the crumbling infrastructure and housing options have led to a decline in residential population. The construction of the Eastern Metropolitan Bypass and its east-west linkages via connector roads, in addition to the extension of the Metro service in the southern parts of the city have bettered accessibility of the eastern and southern wards to the rest of the city. Enhanced communication routes in these areas of the city, together with expanding housing options that are relatively affordable to the middle classes have led to population growth in these parts of Kolkata (Shaw 2016). These demographic changes have recast spatial notions of respectability, danger, and safety in the city, which impinge on everyday mobilities in Kolkata.

Despite rising levels of literacy and education, working-class men in the city are cut off from well-paying jobs in the formal sector and find that the only employment opportunities available to them continue to be insecure jobs in the transport, construction, and petty trading sectors (Gooptu 2007). Moreover, they find themselves in situations where women in their families are better placed to undertake the role of breadwinning. Recent studies show that there has been a surge in the number of single women who migrate to the city from the hinterlands for domestic work; family migration too is increasingly being led not by men's jobs but by women's employment in the informal domestic economy (Sen and Sanyal 2015). Here, we are well served by insights into the character of *bhadralok* patriarchy that infuses gender relations in Bengal. As Ray and Qayum (2009) remind us, the *bhadralok* is a man of culture and education who uses his caste and class privilege to dislodge his male responsibilities as protector and provider of his home. These standards of hegemonic masculinity in the region are impossible for working-class men to match in an urban economic climate where even a factory or office job is exceedingly difficult to find and keep. In *Chippa* (2019), an independent film set in Kolkata, a street child has a chance encounter with a young Bihari taxi driver at night. He tells the driver it must be a lot of fun to drive around the city at night with a cool breeze in your face. The driver replies that it sort of is, but when you have to send money back to your village every month for your wife and child, the fun disappears. Working-class men increasingly find themselves in an urban milieu that makes it ever more difficult for them to be providers. Many feel disadvantaged in relation not just to middle-class men but also to women and shut out from the new economic spaces that have opened in Kolkata. These spaces are projected, in advertisements and billboards in the city's landscape, as particularly hospitable to women. Such visual narratives imply that the new Indian woman—who now even works night shifts—has privileged access to technical and higher education, corporate careers, and greater autonomy in the urban labor market (Paul 2013).

Indeed, one effect of liberalization in India has been the growth of new work opportunities for lower-middle-class women in sectors such as beauty parlors, hotels, hospitals, and malls (Shaw 2012). In these changed circumstances, some local men who are unable to access such opportunities use tactics of intimidation in urban neighborhoods to extort money and engage in petty crimes to make a living. Thus, they may extract payments from neighborhood hawkers, real estate developers, and new residents, deal in illegal liquor, and steal electricity (Gooptu 2007). Such extractive male behavior in urban neighborhoods coexists with pastoral support that young men extend in their localities, largely through the activities of neighborhood clubs. These all-male clubs, ubiquitous in Kolkata's middle-class neighborhoods, informally offer a range of social services, from health and educational drives to organizing funerals and weddings for those unable to afford such expenditures; to the extent that these clubs harbor a sense of ownership of neighborhood space, they also provide security to the localities in which they are embedded.

Such practices embody the desire to be acknowledged and respected as an adult male with influence over the locality (Gooptu 2007). Autorickshaw drivers, in being operators of a primarily neighborhood form of public transport, are a part of such a moral and cultural habitus. A middle-class woman in her early forties described an episode in which an elderly male passenger sitting next to the autorickshaw driver suddenly took ill and fell out of the moving vehicle. The driver pulled over and along with the three other passengers came to the help of the man. The driver decided to take the man to the hospital. When this woman offered him the fare for her ride up to that point, he refused, saying that he had been unable to get her to her destination so it would not be right for him to accept payment. Some weeks later she ran into this driver on the street and asked what happened to the man who had fallen unconscious. He told her that nurses at the hospital had found some numbers on his mobile phone and contacted his family. This book showcases spaces of urban mobility as venues in which men cultivate ethical personhoods. It emphasizes the everyday moralities that pattern interactions between men and genders in the city. In what way does this approach contribute to how gendered lives in cities are understood? To convey a clear sense of the intellectual goals of this book, its placement within feminist urban studies requires some discussion.

Feminist Interventions in Urban Studies

The literature on gender, sexuality, and city spaces in South Asia displays two key motivations. One cluster of studies (Phadke 2005, 2007; Desai 2007; Ranade 2007; Viswanath and Mehrotra 2007; Paul 2011; Pilot and Prabhu 2012; Dhillon and Bakaya 2014) has focused centrally on the question of women's access to public space and the resources of urban living. Making use of feminist scholarship on women and cities in the west (Bondi and Rose 2003; Oswin 2008; Parker 2011), such studies have demonstrated how women in urban India regularly negotiate the sexism in built environments, mores of respectability, and the risk of male sexual violence by employing various strategies of self-preservation, each time they are on city streets. A safety audit of railways stations, conducted in Kolkata by two women's organizations (Parichiti and Jagori 2012), found that several basic amenities—drinking water, toilets for women, waiting areas, travel-related information, facilities for the differently abled, adequate street lighting, and so on— were absent; this had serious implications for women's feelings of safety in such spaces of commuting. Feminists writing on women and cities in contemporary India have pointed out that women's restricted access to public space is to be seen in the context of widespread anxieties surrounding the sexualization of the public sphere. Programmatic moral policing drives, carried out by the cultural right, have therefore increasingly sought to cleanse not just public spaces but the public sphere at large of heterosexual intimacy outside of marriage (Brosius 2013). In what has become an influential claim, it's been suggested that demanding the freedom for women to "loiter" and "risk pleasure" in public spaces constitutes a powerful rupture of patriarchal discourses of femininity that restrict women's participation in public life (Phadke 2007; Phadke, Khan, and Ranade 2009).

Shilpa Phadke argues, for example, that "what women need in order to maximise our access to public space as citizens—is not the provision of safety, for even so-called safe environments are not necessarily comfortable for women, but the right to engage risk" (2007, 1516). Given that women continue to be more susceptible to violence from intimates than from strangers, one could turn Phadke's argument around to say that risk is, in fact, an *imposition* on women in the private domain; everyday life for women in families requires a negotiation of the risk of violence at home. It seems to me that a feminist utopian vision of urbanity would not be cities in which every woman can risk pleasure/danger but those in which women's and gender-nonconforming people's inhabitations of public space would not involve any risk of harm on grounds of gender/sexuality. Phadke, Khan, and Ranade (2009; Phadke 2013) further argue that "loitering" as a feminist strategy has the potential to expand women's claim on public spaces. The reasons for this are that loitering does not require the expenditure of money and allows marginalized groups into the streets, thereby upsetting exclusionary definitions of urban order. Loitering, it is claimed, unsettles constructions of femininity that hinge on the good woman / bad woman divide and "makes possible the dream of an inclusive citizenship by disrupting existent hierarchies and refusing to view the claims of one group against the claims of another" (Phadke, Khan, and Ranade 2009, 197).

Women's freedom to loiter in public spaces is partially reliant on changes in gender roles (of both women and men) within the family. Until men equally share the responsibility of housework, women's participation in public life—for work/leisure—will not expand. Srivastava (2012, 24) makes an important point when he says that "there are significant linkages between discourses and ideologies formulated at institutional sites (whether public or private) and behaviors and expectations at non-institutional spaces such as streets and parks." Middle-class women have been able to access spaces of leisure by transferring the burden of housework on working-class women (Scraton and Watson 1998). Thus, even though loitering is put forth as a way of securing all women's right to the city, given the constraints of material resources, it is middle-class women who may be able to wrest such freedoms, and even for such women the odds stacked against the pursuit of purpose-less pleasure are immense. While historically feminist scholarship on the region has focused on gender-based violence in intimate relations, these newer studies shed light on the perils and triumphs of women negotiating patriarchal trappings in the outdoors. More-over, they bring attention to new forms of middle-class feminist activism against sexual violence in public that do not engage with the state but appeal to a neoliberal vocabulary of personal desire, entrepreneurial capacity, and consumer citizenship (Gupta 2016).

Another set of studies—fewer in number—has explored emergent sexual geographies in urban India. These have variously fore-grounded commodity politics in the making of urban heterosexual masculine identities (Srivastava 2004, 2010, 2013) and borrowed insights from queer theory to highlight the articulation of same-sex desires in the heteronormative city (Balachandran 2004; Boyce 2008). Boyce's work (2008) on male-to-male sexualities in Kolkata scrutinizes practices of cruising to demonstrate the play of ambig-uous signs and indeterminate perceptions in men's sexual encoun-ters with other men in public spaces of the city. He argues that instead of seeing the articulation of same-sex desires as being marginal to the sexual life of heteronormative urban spaces, it is more accurate to emphasize that it is their ambiguity (and not their invisibility) that makes possible their expression in a heterosexist city. More recent work (Boyce 2013) on same-sex sexualities in "small-town" India has underscored men's ambivalence to city liv-ing that simultaneously promises sexual freedom and threatens dislocation from the security of kinship ties in the town. Srivas-tava's studies (2004, 2013) of sex clinics in Delhi (which promise cures for a variety of sexual problems) and what he calls "footpath pornography" in Hindi demonstrate the connections between the desire for commodity consumption, masculine anguish, and urban spatial sensibilities. He argues, for instance, that the pornographic literature in Hindi often includes a search for spaces of sexual/ romantic intimacy (which are mostly inaccessible to the urban poor). Moreover, the "cures" offered by these informal sex clinics, Srivastava avers, are to be seen as constituting an alternative knowledge system in the city, which offers the marginalized a semblance of security in an urban experience characterized by the bewildering pulls between official assurances and denials. Shannon Philip's book (2022) demonstrates how young men's masculinity and class identity coalesce in the new spaces of entertainment and mobility in Delhi.

Even as they retain an empirical focus on women, studies on women and cities in South Asia contain what might be called subtextual ideas about urban masculinity. A crucial ethnographic detail, for instance, that has emerged from this literature is that in navigating the city, middle-class women avoid spaces such as bars, roadside tea stalls, taxi stands, certain street corners, and parks— areas frequented particularly by working-class men—as potential sites of male violence (Ranade 2007; Vishwanath and Mehrotra 2007; Paul 2011. The association of particular urban spaces with sexual harassment/violence has, no doubt, been significant in showing that women's perception of danger manifests itself as a fear of space (Tonkiss 2005). However, the neglect of urban spaces as sites of male sociality, work, and friendship has meant that they have been understood solely as a locus of sexual violence. Inadvertently, interactions between genders on city streets have been framed exclusively in a language of hostility. How do men understand the problem of street harassment and rape? Research in South Africa shows that men's responses assume a variety of forms: while some men consider rape to be a problem of masculinity, they do not necessarily think of it as abuse of women (Sikweyiya, Jewkes, and Morrell 2007). The grammar of male animosity has, as yet, remained underexplored in urban research in South Asia, as have other kinds of exchanges between men and women in public spaces of the city, which may be supportive of one another and may even be consensually erotic.

Many middle-class women commuters I interviewed for this book said that several times they witnessed autorickshaw drivers asking male passengers to sit next to them if there was a sole woman passenger in the backseat. They have found autorickshaw drivers to be supportive when they are cramped between two male passengers; drivers will stop the vehicle so that the woman passenger can sit next to them. By retaining a singular focus on hostility, existing feminist research has not taken into account everyday forms of collaboration between genders in city spaces and the joy that mundane interactions between strangers may generate. While the most widely available narrative about urban commuting and encounters with public transport workers is one of enervation, acrimony, and violence, some interactions in the course of everyday mobility in the city may also evoke empathy, might even be sources of enchantment. An elderly middle-class man who takes taxis regularly reflects on news items, such as a driver slapping a passenger, in this way: "I try to understand their psychology. They work very hard the whole day. They probably don't have time to have a good meal. They are constantly worried about not being able to send enough money back home. Their families are pestering them for money. Then if one passenger behaves badly, the driver may restrain his anger. But if that happens again at a short interval, he might well lose control." A middle-aged Bengali woman recalled an encounter with an elderly Sikh taxi driver: He tells her that newer taxi drivers these days don't observe traffic rules and aren't familiar with the shortest routes in the city. He speaks fluent Bangla, and the woman deeply appreciates that he has such facility in the local language. The driver shares that the younger generation in his community does not want to work as taxi drivers. His own children have been to university and want a respectable office job. "By the way, I have read Rabindranath Tagore in Bangla," he tells her abruptly and proceeds to energetically recite a well-known poem, much to her delight. Such moments are far from the conflictual interactions that are commonly understood to characterize gender relations in the city. By underlining the sociality of public transportation, this book spurs thought on how the city is reproduced as a gendered space through not only conflict but also cooperative gestures between strangers. The ethnography presented here captures the gendered emotional and moral vocabularies through which friction is handled and cooperation transacted in the circuits of urban mobility.

The Fieldwork Enterprise

This book then is a search for masculinities in city spaces and the influence of urbanisms on men's lives. How might we produce sociological knowledge about men and masculinities that is conscious of urban processes? As ethnographers, how do we identify and represent the markings of masculinity on the mores of city living?

At the center of this book are two groups of public transport vehicle operators and their interactions with traffic police and commuters. The first of these is autorickshaw drivers. Over a period of eighteen months, I interviewed twenty drivers and conducted participant observation along two autorickshaw routes in the city. I chose one route that connects upper-middle-class neighborhoods in south Kolkata and a second route that links a cluster of lower-middle-class neighborhoods to the commercial areas in the central districts of the city. The chapter on taxi drivers is based on interviews with twenty-five operators who identify as migrants in Kolkata. The discussion on traffic law enforcement draws on these interviews with drivers as well as fifteen interviews with traffic police personnel and participant observation at workshops conducted by the police with transport workers to sensitize them to safe road practices. My ethnographic target population was, therefore, three occupation groups that are entirely male and require these men to spend extended lengths of time in the urban outdoors. Alongside the commonality between their professions, these two groups of transport workers were also chosen keeping in mind the crucial demographic differences between them. While autorickshaw drivers are "local" men and move within a restricted geography, the majority of taxi drivers in Kolkata are migrants from poorer states in eastern India and roam the entirety of the city's landscape as part of their job. The component on traffic law enforcement was dictated by my conversations with transport workers; the role of the police was so prominent in these interactions that it was impossible to exclude them from this research. It became clear that traffic law enforcement would be an indispensable data source for a project that sought to understand the linkages between masculinity, mobility, and urban space.

I entered the field as a middle-class cisgender male researcher who has lived in Kolkata for twenty-six years and used this mode of public transport all of my adult life in the city. My access to autorickshaw drivers was enabled by the routines of sociability that inflect this particular mode of transportation. In Kolkata, it is very common to see male (and, as we shall see in subsequent chapters, women too) passengers develop sociable relations with autorickshaw drivers as a result of repeated encounters between them. In trying to identify potential interviewees, I inserted myself in these spaces of sociability as a way of establishing personal contact with autorickshaw operators. I would spend time at tea stalls near an autorickshaw depot, where drivers and male passengers are often found having a moment's conversation before going on their way. The nature of transport labor directed the kind of ethnographic contact that I was able to establish with drivers. I quickly learned that these men work excruciatingly long hours, seldom taking off more than a day each week, if at all. It was impossible, therefore, to schedule an interview with either an autorickshaw or taxi driver; doing so would mean compromising either their daily income or their meager leisure hours. Hence, I had to conduct my interviews on the move, sitting beside the autorickshaw driver as a passenger would. I went back and forth on the route, speaking to drivers for between one and two hours. Such go-along interviews (Garcia et al. 2012) meant that particular places along our journey naturally served as pegs for memory, in the sense that drivers would pass through a particular area and remember an incident of note that had transpired there.

The different character of the transport labor that taxi drivers are engaged in meant that I had to use a different strategy to familiarize myself with their lives. Taxi drivers are seldom, if ever, available as a collective in the way that autorickshaw drivers are. I could not, therefore, select drivers to interview after casual interaction with a group of them, as I did with autorickshaw operators. The strategy I developed was to hail a taxi as a passenger and have a conversation with the driver en route to my destination. Given that one of the goals of this book is to understand how the experience of migration shapes working-class men's relationship to urban space, it was important that I identify migrant taxi drivers to interview. As a Bengali, I quickly understood from the inflection of the driver's speech if he was also a native speaker of Bangla. I would begin talking very generally about the taxi profession and then introduce myself as an urban researcher interested to understand the gendered urban lives of migrant taxi drivers.

For the chapter on police work, I approached traffic personnel manning the city's streets, explaining my research project and then requesting them to speak to me about their experience. None of them agreed to speak to me on record. Despite the practical difficulties of taking elaborate notes in the midst of busy and noisy streets, I chose not to push them to allow me to record, thinking that this would enable them to narrate their experiences with less hesitation. I also conducted in-depth interviews with twenty persons who use autorickshaws and taxis regularly to commute in Kolkata. I selected passengers occupying disparate social locations with respect to gender, class, community, religion, and ethnicity.

What do we mean by the term "masculinities," and how might ethnographers recognize and represent masculinities? There are three broad rubrics within which "masculinity" operates in scholarly writings: (1) as a conduit of beliefs/norms/discourses about gender-appropriate behavior, (2) as traits differentiating men and women, and (3) as justification of men's social authority (Flood 2002). In social anthropology specifically, there are four distinct approaches to the concept of masculinity: as anything that men do, men's thoughts and actions as significations of gender, the idea that some men are "more manly" than others, and finally as anything that women are not (Gutmann 1997). In this book I selectively combine Connell's (1987) insistence on naming conduct as it is oriented by power in the domain of gender and Hearn's (2004) suggestion that we move from hegemonic masculinity to the hegemony of men. While these two approaches have been read as somewhat distinct (Flood 2002), I see them as complementary. Considerations of masculinity (and hence femininity) become inalienable from men's conduct because so much of what men do is imbued with ideologies of masculinity. Nevertheless, it is important to bear in mind Eve Sedgwick's (1995) reminder that not everything that men do is about masculinity. The key hermeneutic strategy in this study is to carefully isolate such practices and speech acts in which the meanings of manhood are at stake. Interpretations of masculinities in this project are concerned with (1) practices and speech acts through which male-identified persons signify their gendered selves and (2) their relation to the reproduction of gender inequality in cities. Such an interpretive venture complicates the widely shared assumption that men, particularly cisgender, heterosexual men, are privileged to not think about themselves as gendered. The analyses in the following chapters show that this is not pervasively true; it would be more accurate to say that when men reflect on the meanings of masculinity, they do not necessarily consider issues of gendered power. Moreover, my analyses show that in the instances where questions of masculinity are not foregrounded by men in their speech and actions, social expectations of masculinity continue to underpin men's dwellings in urban space. The sociological task, therefore, has been to identify the interlocking of ideologies of masculinity with the making of everyday life in cities to demonstrate the manner in which the process of becoming men is simultaneous with the production of urban sociality.

Ethnographic writing on the everyday city has to accommodate the fragmentary nature of both the mundane and the urban. Theorists of the everyday have suggested that attending to the quotidian requires thinking about aesthetic forms and expressive genres that can compellingly illuminate the mundane. In its very ordinariness, the everyday tends to escape critical representation, and hence practices of sociological writing must deploy artistic techniques that can defamiliarize the mundane (Highmore 2001). The methodological and interpretive strategy of this book is to combine the rewards of extended participant observation with the benefits of "surface reading." Best and Marcus (2009, 9) write that surfaces entail "what is evident, perceptible, apprehensible . . . what is neither hidden nor hiding. . . . A surface is what insists on being looked at rather than what we must train ourselves to see through." The urban ethnography presented in the following chapters attends in this manner to the surfaces of the everyday city. The fleeting character of quotidian mobility in city spaces, even when it assumes a somewhat tenuous structure, offers itself to both habitués and urban researchers primarily as a surface. To harness the ethnographic mode such that it can render urbanism legible, I expended time in the field and sought to cultivate a poetics of writing that can capture, in fragments, the phenomenological patterns of everyday urban mobilities. This is by no means an exceptional venture. The legacy of the "writing culture" intervention in anthropology rests substantially on attentiveness to ethnography as a rhetorical practice. This book seeks to know the city not just through the steadiness of immersive participation but also through descriptions and anecdotes that illuminate even though they flicker. As Fran Tonkiss (2005, 128) reminds us, "the city comes to us in bits and pieces."

Structure of the Book

The street has long been a subject of sociological investigation. Thought to encapsulate social encounters that are emblematic of urban life, the street has been studied simultaneously as a site of social prejudice and one of social change (Hubbard and Lyon 2018). This book takes the street as a site of flows in which everyday movements become a domain for the production of gendered identities. It identifies ambition/disappointment, friction/collaboration, crime/safety, fear/pleasure, mobility/stillness, power/vulnerability, and right/wrong as the principal dyads through which working-class men navigate the city. The project unfolds through five chapters. In the first, I lay out the broad social and policy context within which public transportation in Kolkata operates and sketch a contemporary history of urbanization and mobility patterns in the region. Following this, three chapters narrate the gendered lives of autorickshaw operators, taxi drivers, and traffic police in the city, respectively. The fifth chapter gathers some recurring themes from the preceding discussions to spotlight the city as a space of moral becoming.

The discussion of the cartographies of autorickshaw drivers adopts a micro-sociological approach to unravel this mode of neighborhood transit as a sociable infrastructure that variously hinders and facilitates the accomplishment of masculine identities. Ethnographic attention to forms of copresence on the autorickshaw reveals that transport infrastructures engender rituals of cooperation and conflict through which the gendered social order of the city is produced. Skirmishes between driver and commuter frequently invoke ideas of uncivil working-class masculinity that are considered to be at variance with the image of the city that is desired by the urban middle class. These clashes notwithstanding, the associational life of the autorickshaw simultaneously deepens awareness of social difference and manufactures bonds of neighborliness in the city. Mothers of children who go to the same school may chitchat in the autorickshaw. Through these chats, they may learn of a good teacher who offers private lessons to students. Sometimes they will pay the other's fare, as a friendly gesture. These bonds are a resource for both passengers and drivers and allow them to relish the pleasure of urban sociability. By bringing the literature on urban infrastructure in conversation with masculinity studies, this chapter uncovers the interface between cultures of masculinity and the social life of mobility through which infrastructural space is inhabited in the city.

Chapter 3, on taxi driving, moves from the scale of the neighborhood to the city at large. Through this scalar shift, this chapter highlights the relative power that frames men's interactions with other men in the city and the distinctly spatial basis of these relations. It traces entanglements of masculinity and mobility by considering how experiences of rural-to-urban migration, crime and safety, desire and pleasure, and risk frame working-class men's labor geographies in the city. For taxi drivers, as migrants living away from their wives, sexual desire becomes a specific kind of problematic in their city lives, and this chapter shows the erotic urban topography that migrant male heterosexuality generates. Furthermore, the nature of cab driving produces the migrant taxi operator as a vulnerable urban subject who is exposed to the vagaries of strangers and unpredictable cartographies of movement. The indeterminacy of the modern city, this chapter submits, makes men's experiences of risk assume a particular character: in patriarchal cultures, men have to show a readiness to risk themselves, a willingness to take on dangerous tasks. The city, in its expansive unknowability, emerges as the primary arena for men's risky behavior; it presents men with the opportunity to prove that they can tackle threats to body and masculine identity without being daunted by the prospect of urban danger. As one taxi driver said, "I roam the streets all day and night, deal with whatever they throw at me; the city teaches me things a pen pusher will never know."

In being a part of the city's informal economy, taxi drivers and autorickshaw operators are repeatedly brought into conflict with traffic police, who question their right to labor in the city. The next chapter, on traffic law enforcement, draws on anthropological literature on the everyday state to identify how cultures of masculinity on city streets inflect state regulation of urban mobilities. Even though many of the interactions between traffic police and transport workers are rooted in friction, as men they also share with each other a tacit understanding of the social compulsions of masculinity. Time and again I heard traffic police caution drivers that they should observe traffic rules because if their license were to be rescinded, they would not be able to earn a living and provide for their families. Men's roles within the family, as sons, husbands, and fathers, as well as the naturalization of male heterosexual desire, provide a gendered logic of cooperation between traffic police and transport workers. These logics are captured in the concept of "homosocial trust" that this chapter offers. As a heuristic, the homosociality of everyday trust tracks the cooperative gestures and moral inflections of the everyday state through which urban mobility is governed and inhabited.

In a short film released in 2012 titled *Calcutta Taxi*, a taxi driver helps a man chase down another taxi that has run away with his bag, only to get embroiled with a protesting crowd and beaten up by traffic police. The taxi driver is seen explaining to his young helper that while honesty is a good thing, it often does not help those who practice it; nevertheless, one still ought to act honestly. In the same film, another taxi driver confesses to his newly married wife that he has a hearing impairment and does not want his marriage to be built on dishonesty when throughout his life as a taxi driver he has always acted ethically with his customers. A theme that implicitly runs through this book is everyday morality. The social life of public transportation is permeated by moral considerations. Moral values impinge on the interactions that inhere in these spaces, moral vocabularies are used by everyday actors to make sense of urban mobility, and the act of trusting someone or withholding trust construes people as distinct moral subjects. Taking an anecdotal approach drawn from literary theories, the fifth chapter foregrounds the workings of morality in the circuits of commuting by identifying a cast of urban characters. The word "character" refers to persons in a fictional world as well as to the mental and moral traits that distinguish individuals. The ethnographic stories through which urban characters come alive provide a narrative structure to how men make moral sense of copresence in the mobile city. Recognizing these character types highlights the role of ordinary morality in the gendered making of the urban social. In interactions on public transport, the private worlds of family and intimacy are interlocked with the public worlds of labor and urban sociability. By telling stories of everyday urban characters, this chapter shows how the gendered subjectivities that inhere in commuting spaces are shaped by logics of private morality.

Men's lives in the city *as men* have seldom been examined in urban studies. Although the idea that formations of masculinity are spatially contingent has seen much discussion (Jackson 1991; Longhurst 2000; Berg and Longhurst 2003), this insight—besides a handful of exceptions (Sommers 1998; Kenway and Hickey-Moody 2009; Lumsden 2013; Parker 2017)—has seldom provoked sustained attention to the specifically urban ramifications of masculinities. This is a serious lacuna because urbanization processes are closely tied to the identity work that men perform as social subjects. A fuller understanding of these connections requires studies that engage with a range of urban processes in relation to ideas of masculinity. The ethnography reported in this book suggests that much of the conflict and insecurity that men experience in the city is bound up with paid work and heteronormative gendered roles in the family being the primary bases of male self-esteem in patriarchal cultures. Men's feelings of insecurity in the city are about the loss of economic and social authority to other men and to women. The city is the principal space where men may prove their manhood through gainful employment and successfully dislodge their responsibility as providers for their families; but rising economic insecurity and the dominance of middle-class values in shaping the urban mean that the city, especially for working-class men, is simultaneously the site of their greatest failure.

Despite the many skirmishes and violations that pervade everyday urban interactions, how do men and women repose an element of trust in strangers as they traverse the city? This book argues that everyday morality and gendered logics of cooperation help us to understand what holds together the urban social. In the city as a community of strangers, mundane moral assessments of people, times, and places are a mode of identifying danger and support, conflict and cooperation, appropriate and wrongful conduct, the fickle and the reliable. In this sense, the geographies of public transport are a practical workshop in which urban dwellers construct moral personhoods both for themselves and for others. The moral values and norms that people leverage to manage copresence on public transportation are prisms for what different urban social groups consider the good city to be. The moral filter through which copresence in the city becomes discernible to inhabitants is fundamentally gendered in the sense that the moral exaltation of gender roles in the heteronormative family supplies the interpretive framework to adjudicate between the good and the bad, the appropriate and the improper in city living. The influence of private morality on city interactions partially explains the ideological association between the urban outdoors, men, and masculinity. The emphasis on everyday morality facilitates the empirically derived argument made in this book for shifting feminist interpretation of urban life away from an exclusive preoccupation with violence and pleasure to the gendered nature of social collaboration in cities. Through this invitation to consider the collaborative character of gendered city making, this book suggests that feminist insights into the masculinist city are enhanced when rituals of urban cooperation are brought within the ambit of analysis. Mundane gestures of support between and among genders make the city livable for urban inhabitants but also prepare the ideological ground for serious conflicts, including violence, to erupt between them. By unveiling such collaboration in the everyday usage of public transport services in Kolkata—and disruptions to it—this book offers an understanding of how cities reproduce themselves as spaces of patriarchal power.

1

The Urban Landscape
of Public Transport

The relations between masculinities, mobilities, and urban spaces, which this book tracks, are embedded in a wider context of urbanization processes and gendered labor configurations in the region. To sufficiently understand how masculinities matter in the social life of urban public transport, this chapter sketches the broader social and policy frames that shape everyday mobilities in Kolkata. Before establishing close ethnographic contact with the lives of male transport workers who are at the center of this book, this chapter traces Kolkata's experiments with everyday mobility and public transport provisioning. In offering this overview of urban transport services and recent transformations in urban culture in the region, the chapter identifies analytical routes for making sense of the links between masculinity, mobility, and city life.

Public Transportation in Urban India

Postcolonial urban scholarship has critiqued the imperialism of epistemological frameworks, which persistently read cities of the Global South solely as exemplars of developmental problems (A. Roy 2011). It is difficult, however, to narrate a story of India's public transport situation without reference to the congestion, road fatalities, accidents, environmental hazards, affordability, reliability, noise, and issues of access that make up everyday realities of urban commuting. Indeed, laying out these problems would help identify the practices through which urban actors make the city livable for them despite these mobility challenges. Ethnographic research on traffic and congestion in non-Western cities such as Istanbul (Yazici 2013) and Jakarta (Lee 2015) has recuperated these urban problems as sites where subjectivities are fashioned, social relations negotiated, and skills of urban survival cultivated. The ubiquity of traffic snarls in Indian megacities like Bangalore, for instance, has led scholars to suggest that the congestion of mobility infrastructures in southern cities is better conceived as a process of improvisation and repair (Gopakumar 2015). If everyday congestion on city roads is not simply a technical phenomenon but also socially meaningful, it becomes relevant to consider—as the following chapters in this book do—how urban traffic is inscribed by ideas of gender and masculinity.

The speedy pace of urbanization in South Asia, coupled with the growing influx of people into cities, has intensified travel demand within cities in the region. Estimates show that the total number of daily passenger trips in eighty-seven urban centers in India will increase from approximately 229 million in 2007 to 482 million in 2031 (Pucher et al. 2005). In Lahore, Pakistan, different forms of public transport cumulatively carry some 800,000 passengers a day, and between 2001 and 2008 motorcycle ownership increased by 483 percent (Ahmad, Batool, and Starkey 2019). These high travel numbers in the region, however, have not seen a commensurate upgrade of transport infrastructure, and most transport facilities for intracity travel continue to be used much in excess of their capacity. The road fatality rate in urban India grew from thirty-six fatalities per million persons in 1980 to ninety-five per million in 2006 (Mohan et al. 2009). The autorickshaw, on account of its lower weight and small engine size, is associated with a lower risk of road deaths and injuries (Goel 2018). One major factor explaining the rise in road mishaps is the vast growth in private motor vehicles in cities. In India, the liberalization of the car industry began in the 1970s, and the sector was entirely de-licensed in 1993. This led to rapid internationalization, with an increasing number of multinational car manufacturers entering the market (Tetzlaff 2017). The popularity of the private car bears relation to it being an emblem of social status among the middle and upper classes (Nielsen and Wilhite 2017). Little is known, however, about how different vehicles function as conduits of masculinity in urban spaces in India.

The coexistence of different types of motorized vehicles with nonmotorized forms of intracity travel gives rise to mixed traffic flow conditions, which frequently produce conflict between different people who are moving through the city at different paces. Speaking about order maintenance in public spaces in Indian cities, Bayley (1969, 260) mentions the "violence of frustration" wherein "commuters on trams or trains have sometimes smashed vehicles, burned trams, stopped trains, and beaten official personnel because there was a breakdown on the line or their train was shunted to one side to allow a faster train to pass." This book asks in what ways gender contributes to the production of this frustration on city streets and how gendered ideals mitigate some of this everyday conflict on public transport. It must be said that there are vast differences in the travel behaviors between those living in urban slums and those in formal housing. For slum dwellers, cycling and walking compose between 50 and 75 percent of commuter trips (Tiwari 2007). This mobility trend resonates with patterns in other South Asian countries: in Pakistan, for example, as much as 95 percent of daily mobility among both men and women is nonmotorized and the percentage of automobile trips is directly proportional to income, especially among women (Adeel, Gar-On Yeh, and Zhang 2016). Given that most of India's urban poor are unable to afford even the lowest public transport fares, the field of public transport infrastructure within Indian cities becomes a contact zone between commuters belonging to the middle classes and transport workers who are male and working class.

In 1981 there were about 5.4 million vehicles registered in the country. This number grew to 21.4 million in 1991, 54.9 million in 2001, and 141 million in 2011 (Valeur 2014). In reflecting on these numbers, it is important to note the high concentration of private vehicles in just a handful of cities in the country. About 32 percent of private vehicles in India are in cities alone, which house merely 11 percent of the whole country's population (Pucher et al. 2005). In 2010 the "Accidents, Deaths and Suicides in India" section of the National Crime Records Bureau in India recorded that 133,938 people had lost their lives in road traffic accidents. Statistics compiled by the Ministry of Road Transport and National Highways suggest that traffic fatalities grew by nearly 5 percent between 1980 and 2000 and by 8 percent in the next four years. To the extent that public transportation in cities connects people to their homes, education, work, and leisure and medical facilities, it constitutes a key element in urban dwellers' experience of city living. The sheer preponderance of road accidents, of varying scales of severity, in Indian cities has naturalized this kind of urban danger; it is seen as an unavoidable hazard of urban life. The chapters that follow identify some ways in which masculinity inflects the everyday management of urban danger in Indian cities.

Autorickshaws in Indian cities function mostly as a cheaper alternative to the taxi. In providing first and last mile connectivity, they ensure that urban citizens are able to access public transport facilities (Mohan and Roy 2003). Given that public transportation does not usually accommodate door-to-door connectivity, autorickshaws fulfil this need and, in doing so, take away from the need to rely on private cars to meet door-to-door connectivity. In Kolkata, since the autorickshaw is a shared mode of transport, this door-to-door function is not easily dispensed. Nevertheless, with the multiplication of their routes and their reach into the inner localities of neighborhoods, in Kolkata too autorickshaws approximate to an extent the door-to-door function they serve in other Tier 1 Indian cities. Estimates reveal the market size of autorickshaws to be between 15,000 and 30,000 in Tier 2 cities (that is, those that have a population between one and four million) and more than 50,000 in Tier 1 cities (population more than four million) (Mani et al. 2012). Surveys on the use of autorickshaws in these cities suggest that they have between four and sixteen of them for every one thousand people. The production of autorickshaws doubled between 2003 and 2010. There are some 147,000 registered autos in Bangalore, 69,309 in Mumbai, and 70,000 in Delhi (Mani et al. 2012).

Urbanization patterns are, of course, related to land-use patterns. In India, the growth of cities has caused a spatial spread outward. This sprawled development has extended the boundaries of the city. Such expansion has inadvertently increased average trip lengths, forced dependency on motorized forms of transport, and made walking and cycling even less feasible (Tiwari 2007). Such growth patterns have necessitated increases to bus fleets, but the increases have been slower than the growth of private vehicle ownership. Estimates show that the total number of buses quadrupled between 1981 and 2002, whereas the number of motorcycles and cars in Indian cities grew by sixteen times and seven times, respectively (Mohan 2013). The chapters that follow trace the contestations of masculinity as they are articulated through the flows of dissimilar speeds of mobility in the city.

To the extent that public transport is a state subject according to the Indian constitution, until 2006 the central government did not have a unified policy for urban transport infrastructure. The idea was that city governments would devise their own strategies for resolving their transport crises. State governments across the country have invested a great deal of capital to widen roads to ease congestion; but as Tiwari (2007) argues, these measures benefit only personal vehicle users. In 2004, however, a national urban transport policy was drafted and adopted two years later. The Jawaharlal Nehru National Urban Renewal Mission (JNNURM) was introduced to grapple with the dire state of infrastructure in Indian cities. The mission listed sixty-three cities that were to receive assistance from the central government to upgrade their road infrastructure. This mission also provided a set of recommendations for upgrading public transport facilities in these cities. In order to get approval for their transport projects, the guidelines required state governments to follow the National Urban Transport Policy (NUTP), issued in 2006. In response to the pervasiveness of gender-based violence and harassment on city streets, the NUTP recommended a number of measures to tackle this problem and enhance women's commuting experience. These included police-verified drivers and conductors in buses and paratransit modes of intracity travel, CCTV cameras in all bus and train terminals as well as audiovisual passenger information system, and emergency alarm systems in all public transport vehicles. The NUTP also highlighted the importance of street design in making cities safer for women, through providing proper lighting and avoiding dead ends in street planning.

Since the end of JNNURM in 2014, the government of India has initiated the Atal Mission for Rejuvenation and Urban Trans-formation (AMRUT). With a budget of INR500 billion over a five-year period, AMRUT covers areas of urban intervention such as water infrastructure, public transport, and urban greening in five hundred Indian cities. Since becoming prime minister in 2014, Narendra Modi and his party have also put forth the Smart Cities Mission (SCM), with the objective of creating smart cities using information and communication technology, public-private part-nerships, and private-sector investment. The announcement was made in June 2015 to develop one hundred smart cities, with INR4,800 crore being allocated toward this goal. The Urban Green Mobility Scheme in 2017 aims to promote sustainable urban mobil-ity by enhancing nonmotorized transport and buses, moving to electric vehicles for public transport, and providing alternates to fos-sil fuels (Joshi et al. 2021). Urban commentators have argued that the smart cities initiative is a thoroughly elitist project geared toward private capital accumulation with the goal of using technology to merely avoid and not address problems of urban informality and climate adaptation (Hoelscher 2016).

Kolkata's Public Transportation Landscape

The Kolkata Metropolitan Area (KMA) is India's third largest—after Mumbai and Delhi—with respect to population size. Located in eastern India, in the state of West Bengal, the KMA has an area of 1,886.67 km². The 2011 census reports its population to be 14.11 million (Shaw 2015). The public transport landscape of Kolkata offers the following options to its inhabitants: buses (state and private), taxis, autorickshaws, cycle rickshaws, hand-pulled rickshaws, trams, ferries, suburban railways, and the metro. All transport workers in Kolkata, without exception, are men. Reports show that the extent of public transport usage is highest in Kolkata among all India cities. Of all trips in Kolkata, 80 percent use public transport, while the figures for Mumbai, Chennai, and Delhi are 60, 42, and 42 percent, respectively (Pucher et al. 2005).

The Calcutta State Transport Corporation (CSTC) was established in 1948 and began operations with a fleet of twenty-five buses. A reason why CSTC was established was to provide employment, especially for refugees, and not to provide urban transport. In 1988, CSTC had 1,266 buses covering eighty routes; in 1990, there were 3,000 private buses and 900 minibuses (Sen 2016). In July 2014, a number of air-conditioned buses were launched by CSTC, which currently cover forty different routes across the city. In an autobiographical piece on her experience of the "crush of people who board the buses" in Kolkata, historian Janaki Nair (2014, 54) writes that no other public transport system in any other Indian city would countenance passengers traveling without paying the fare right until the very last moment before they disembark. She suggests that this lenience has to do with the unreliability of bus services in the city.

Surveys show that there are nearly two million cycle rickshaws in India's cities, ferrying between six and eight billion passengers every year (Samanta and Roy 2013). In Kolkata, the innumerable interior lanes—too narrow for heavier vehicles—are architecturally suitable for rickshaws, both hand-pulled and pedaled. The hand-pulled rickshaw—governed by the Calcutta Hackney Carriage Act of 1919—has frequently been the recipient of state intervention and social commentary in that it is seen as a primitive form of labor that contravenes both individual dignity and the image of a modern city. From the early 1980s, the state government has made successive attempts to phase out the presence of hand-pulled

rickshaws by removing unlicensed rickshaws and refusing to issue license renewals. That these steps coincided with the introduction and expansion of autorickshaws in the city is certainly not incidental. In Kolkata, the majority of rickshaw pullers are Hindi-speaking migrants from Bihar. A survey conducted by the Kolkata Samaritan suggests that nearly 66 percent of rickshaw pullers migrated from Bihar, 17 percent from Jharkhand, and another 17 percent from rural West Bengal and Bangladesh (Samanta and Roy 2013). Approximately half of them live on the streets, while the other half share the smallest of rooms with several others; a few of them manage to find a place in the verandahs of the rich by rendering services like picking up children from school or running small errands. As the architectural landscape of the city changes and old houses with *rowaks* and extended balconies on the ground floor make way for vertical forms of urban dwelling, taking recourse to such makeshift forms of subsistence is becoming rare, and many rickshaw pullers now live in the very carriages that they use to ferry passengers (Das 2004). Since the 1980s, the state government has tried to substitute poor migrant workers with local unemployed youth in the transport sector. This contemporary history is important to underline because it highlights the relationships of conflict that migrant men are brought into with so-called local men in the urban transport sector of the state. The state's efforts notwithstanding, there are still about eighteen thousand hand-pulled rickshaws in the city whose pullers earn about INR8,000 to 10,000 per month.

Calcutta Metro, India's first underground railway project, started operation in 1984. Until 2010, when new stations were added, the metro ran from Dumdum in the north to Tollygunj in the south, for a length of 16.45 kilometers, which is covered in thirty minutes (Roy 1990). In its current state, the metro network comprises a single operational line measuring 38.6 kilometers, which runs from the north to the south of the city. Several other lines and stations are in the process of being constructed. The total passenger count in 2001 was 630 million (Singh 2002). There hasn't been much research on the gendered aspects of metro travel in Kolkata, but feminist perspectives on Delhi's metro system provide some crucial insights. While the metro in Delhi was seen as a much safer option of travel for women in its early days, facilitating them to create a private domain in shared public space, in more recent years, with increasing cases of sexual harassment and overcrowding, new contestations around gender and commuting have emerged (Sadana 2010). Many men consider the metro to be a space for potentially romantic interactions with women, which the introduction of coaches reserved for women impedes and hence is resented (Agrawal and Sharma 2015). While sex-segregated coaches were introduced on Delhi's metro to provide physical safety for women commuters, many women reported an increase in men's hostility toward them after this reservation policy was implemented.

The Kolkata Suburban Railway system serves the suburbs surrounding the city, connecting them to each other and to the capital city. Ananya Roy's (2003) well-known study of the gender of poverty in Kolkata reads the suburban railway in the region as a rural-urban interface constituted through the commuting of everyday migrants, especially the rural landless. In the geographies of these women who commute from southern villages to middle-class neighborhoods in Kolkata, using the suburban train compartments teeming with people, Roy reads a disruption of the binaries of public/private and rural/urban. In the women-only compartments, these poor women eke out the benefit of ticketless travel, using their gender to evade the regulatory presence of male ticket checkers. Roy notes that on these commuter trains, when poor working women speak of unemployed men connected to them through affinal ties, their vocabulary presents male unemployment as a marker of sexual incapability and disempowerment. The subjects of Roy's book are poor women who are primary earners in their families. These women are migrants in the city or daily commuters to it whose low levels of household income are explained partially by men's inability or refusal to contribute to the family's subsistence or by their abandonment of their families.

The subjects of this book are the men who stay; it is about the men who constitute their gendered personhoods through a set of ethical ideas about their labor, the city of their toil, and family life. While Roy offers an understanding of the feminization of livelihood when women become principal earners, my project considers the relation between male transport workers' ethical commitment to their jobs, their social roles as men, and the masculinization of city spaces.

AUTORICKSHAWS

The autorickshaw was incorporated into the public transport landscape of Kolkata in 1983. It was brought in as part of the self-employment scheme as a way of addressing pervasive youth unemployment in the city. Thus, while taxi and hand-pulled rickshaw operators in the city have, historically, mostly been from outside West Bengal, the bus, minibus, and autorickshaw segments of the transport industry have a vast majority of Bengali workers. In a similar trend, the Indonesian city of Surabaya has seen the traditional *becak* replaced by the motorbike taxi that simultaneously provides a form of urban transportation and work opportunity for underemployed men (Peters 2020). In present-day Kolkata, nearly half of all autorickshaw drivers also own the vehicles they drive; the rest pay a daily rent to the owner. In 1987, the number of registered autorickshaws was 1,865. The number of registered autos plying the KMA in 2001 was 22,000 (Dutta 2015) and shot up to 46,000 by 2020.

Autorickshaws began with what was called the "Calcutta Permit," which allowed them to transport passengers throughout the city, in the manner of taxis. The need to regulate their geography, however, emerged quickly, and soon the "North-South Permit" was introduced. This permit restricted the movement of autorickshaws to either the northern or southern regions of the city; those with a permit from one region were disallowed from traveling to the other region (Paul 2015). This was followed by the Block Permit, which further restricted their geography within the jurisdiction of particular police stations. In present-day Kolkata, unlike other Tier 1 cities, autos ply within designated routes and on a shared basis, an arrangement that started in the late 1990s. Estimates from 2015 show that 50 percent of autorickshaw routes traverse a distance of three to eight kilometers, while 40 percent cover three to five kilometers. Although only 125 routes are officially registered, in practice well over 180 routes operate (Dutta 2015).

The income profile of autorickshaw drivers in Kolkata is as follows: Approximately 58 percent of them bring in between INR5,000 and 10,000 every month; some 17 percent earn between INR10,000 and 15,000. Nonowner drivers have to pay approximately INR300 every day as rent to the owner. Daily fuel expenses amount to INR250. Most drivers work at least twelve hours per day, on a six-day schedule; many drive every day and take breaks only when unavoidable. Only about 30 percent of drivers have at least a primary education. Surveys of auto operators in Kolkata suggest that the majority are Bengali, Hindu, middle-aged, married men. Some 39 percent are between twenty-six and thirty-five years, while 31 percent are between thirty-six and forty-five. Approximately

80 percent are Hindu, with a little over 60 percent falling among the general castes. Of drivers, 16.5 percent are Hindi speakers. Over 80 percent are married (Sen 2016).

It is estimated that in the KMA in 2001, the number of passengers using transport services was approximately 117,000; the figure for 2011 was 1,40,00,000. Survey research on the income profile of autorickshaw passengers in Kolkata reveals a telling picture. This mode of transport serves some 50,00,000 individuals. An estimated 23 percent of passengers fall in the income range of INR10,000 to 15,000 per month; approximately 22 percent earn between INR15,000 and 20,000; 17 percent fall between INR20,000 and 30,000. These data must be seen in the light of what is known about the earning capacity of bus passengers: 43.5 percent of them earn below INR2,000 per month, and 33 percent earn between INR2,000 and 5,000 (Dutta 2015). Thus, compared with regular bus passengers, those who use the autorickshaw to commute are a part of India's middle class. It is also worth remembering that in Indian cities 30 percent of households earn less than INR5,000 per month. Those whose income capacities fall in this range do not have the means to pay for public transport for short distances; they usually walk or ride bicycles. In the KMA, 60 percent of daily trips are within three kilometers. According to available data, some 35,00,000 passengers commuted daily on autorickshaws in 2001; the figure for 2011 was 47,00,000 (Dutta 2015).

The popularity of the autorickshaw as a mode of transport despite pervasive discontentment with its operators has to do with how it compares with other forms of transportation available to the urban commuter. The autorickshaw is convenient in that it can be hailed at any point on the road, is not overcrowded like the bus and metro, and has a vehicular design that is much more accommodative of older people and those with mobility problems (Sen 2016). Moreover, they are available to commuters for fares that the middle class can afford on a daily basis. This situation is at variance with that in a city like Dhaka in neighboring Bangladesh, where 37 percent of total trips are made using busses, which people above the age of sixty are dependent on because of their affordability relative to other modes such as autorickshaws and taxis (Jahangir et al. 2022). Autorickshaw users in Dhaka are frequently victims of purse snatchings, which raises the issue of personal safety while commuting. Nationally in India, the distribution of buses in the urban transport landscape has reduced significantly, from 11 percent of the total fleet in 1951 to 1.1 percent in 2001. In Kolkata, many middle-income commuters have shifted from the bus to the autorickshaw.

The awkward legal status of the autorickshaw in India invites consideration. The autorickshaw has no place in official law. Even through its many amendments, the Central Motor Vehicles Act avoids all reference to the autorickshaw. This absence from a central act that has legal applicability throughout the country coexists with discussions of legal provisions pertaining to the autorickshaw in the West Bengal Motor Vehicles Rules. In yet another instance of urban informality, the presence of autorickshaws has been regularized by state government rules and judicial directives (Sen 2016). For example, the West Bengal Motor Vehicles Act 1980 enjoins the autorickshaw driver to keep a set of documents in the vehicle at all times. These include the permit, insurance certificate, registration certificate, fitness certificate, tax token, driver's license, first-aid box, spare wheel, and toolbox. Then, as per Section 173 of the rules, if the number of passengers exceeds the prescribed limit, both the passenger and the driver will be required to pay a fine. Moreover, no music may be played on the audio system or radio.

It is important to stress that both the registration and permit are notoriously difficult to obtain, besides being very expensive (Sen 2016). Such disincentives have led to more than half of all drivers taking to the trade without the required documentation, and hence there are a large number of unregistered autos. This paralegal status creates a perennial condition of uncertainty for autorickshaw operators as they labor in the city. It is telling that nearly 78 percent of drivers surveyed reported being harassed by traffic police (Sen 2016).

The daily operations of the autos are managed by the auto unions, which exercise considerable influence over who enters the sector; hence personal networks play a vital role in mediating not just who joins the trade but also how disputes that may arise are resolved. Unions also decide fares; but this is my no means a unilateral process. Rather, fares are planned locally for each route (Sen 2016). The autorickshaw has also frequently been placed at the center of discussions and policy interventions on urban pollution. Purportedly in view of the dismal air quality in the city, a division of the Calcutta High Court issued a ruling in July 2008 that required all two-stroke autorickshaws to be converted to four-stroke engines no later than December 31, 2008. At this time some 38,000 vehicles were operating on petrol, while another 30,000 were running on contaminated fuel. This conversion was carried out in the ensuing months, and in December 2009 the West Bengal transport minister confirmed that the court's directive had been implemented. To facilitate the conversion, the state government compensated owners with INR10,000 per vehicle (Dutta 2015). While most drivers now welcome this change because it makes driving a smoother experience, besides being less harmful for the driver's health, they also partially blame the high price of liquefied petroleum gas (LPG) for their reduced incomes.

TAXIS

In 1977 the number of registered taxis in Calcutta was 6,956, which grew to 15,630 by 1987. In the 1990s, taxi permits were relaxed, which led to exponential growth of the number of taxis in the city (Sen 2016). In 2014–2015, there were 60,682 registered taxis in Kolkata. Since the beginning of taxi operations in the city, the trade has been associated with the Sikh community. Today, the vast majority of taxi operators in Kolkata are from Bihar and Jharkhand. It is unclear precisely when this change in the community profile of taxi drivers, from Sikhs to Biharis, began. A comprehensive history of Sikh settlement in Bengal is beyond the scope of this book. Nevertheless, since Bihari taxi drivers in contemporary Kolkata—who are the subjects of this study—are evaluated by the urban public in relation to the dwindling community of Sikh drivers, it is relevant to provide some idea of the latter community's life in the city, especially as it relates to the transport industry.

Taxis began operating in Calcutta in 1907, but Sikhs joined the industry in larger numbers in the early 1920s (Banerjee 2012). The majority of them are landowning Jat-Sikhs, with roots in the Malwa region of Punjab. Himadri Banerjee suggests that their taking up transport work is possibly explained by their experience in driving and performing machine work while serving in the British-Indian Army. They thus gravitated toward the transport sector as Calcutta's surface transport services grew in the early twentieth century. Over time, Sikh taxi drivers acquired a reputation for being honest and reliable, which is perhaps a residual effect of their history of fighting the British in Bengal, their past as defenders of Hindu communities at the time of the Great Calcutta Killing of August 1946, and the soldier-saint ideal of Sikh masculinity in the colonial period. Banerjee further claims that this approbation declined after the 1960s, evidenced by an increasing number of Bengali periodicals in the late twentieth century beginning to ridicule the Sikh community as stupid. This derisive attitude of the Bengali people toward the Sikhs largely coexists with a pervasive feeling that Sikh men are hardworking and honest. As recently as 2016, for instance, a Facebook post reporting an act of honesty by a Sikh taxi driver in Kolkata was shared some nine thousand times and liked by twenty-four thousand profiles within a span of twenty-four hours.

In stark contrast with this image of Sikh honesty, the Bihari taxi driver is mostly described as uncivilized. Newspaper reports repeatedly invoke the figure of the "rogue driver" and decry the "taxi menace" that plagues life in the city. The taxi drivers' faults range from rampant and arbitrary refusal, through quarrelsome behavior, overcharging, and robbery, to different types of assault. A number of allegations of sexual violence toward women have been reported in recent years. For their part, the various taxi associations in West Bengal have regularly initiated strikes, demanding a hike in the fare structure to accommodate rising costs of living. The following comment from the transport minister, Madan Mitra, reported in an English daily, captures the cultural logic that is often levied to explain the Bihari migrant taxi drivers' incivility: "Most of the taxi drivers are not aware of Bengal's language and culture and the sentiment of local people and thus fail to provide them with the service they require."

In attempting to understand the reasons behind the transformation of the community profile of taxi drivers in Kolkata, it is worth dwelling on the various factors that propel male-only outmigration from Bihari to more prosperous states in the country. Bihar has a very long history of out-migration, traceable to the nineteenth century, a time when the region provided indentured laborers for British colonies such as Fiji and the West Indies, in addition to the jute mills of Bengal (Priyadarshini 2014). Studies on contemporary Bihar show that the very low wages in Bihar impel vast numbers of men to migrate, some to the relatively affluent region of central Bihar but mostly to states like West Bengal, Haryana, Punjab, and Maharashtra. Research shows that one in every two households in the region has at least one male member who has migrated without his family (A. K. Roy 2011). Migrants from Bihar also tend to pick work destinations that already have people they know well to help them find jobs there and adjust to a new life. Roy's study shows that 80 percent of the sampled migrants followed either relatives or people they knew from their community. Her research also indicates that approximately 60 percent of migrants first relocated between the ages of fifteen and twenty-five and that most of them return to their homes in Bihar at least once in a year, staying between fifteen and sixty days. Generally speaking, they plan their visits to coincide with the harvest seasons and important festivals. These trends, as we will see in the ensuing chapters, find reflection in the lives of migrant taxi drivers in Kolkata. The majority of migrants from Bihar to Bengal find work in the transport, construction, and service industries, primarily as drivers, watchmen, barbers, washermen, sweepers, and construction workers (A. K. Roy 2011; Jha and Pushpendra 2014).

This pattern of migration and the proximity of Bihar to Kolkata imply that migrant men who come to the city to work as taxi drivers retain intimate connections to their villages. As de Haan (2007) explains, the reason for this pattern of migration in the region has to do with the insecurity of working and living conditions in Kolkata, which contribute significantly to their wish to move back to their villages after retirement. Migrant workers' close links with their village communities are prolonged also by the continuance of agricultural smallholdings in Bihar. In other words, migrants from the state of Bihar use their earnings in cities to maintain their families back home and their roles in agricultural economies, and this involves meeting not just daily household expenses but also the costs of a range of farm activities (A. K. Roy 2011). Nevertheless, while seasonal labor migration from villages in India has mostly been read as a result of extreme economic deprivation, many migrants also consider migration to be a route to temporary freedom from problems at home, an escape from the authority of their parents, or an opportunity to enjoy amorous relationships (Shah 2006).

Uber, the global ride-sharing technology company, began operating in India in the city of Bangalore in 2013. It launched in Kolkata on August 19, 2014. Until then, the yellow-black and yellow ambassador taxi had a monopoly over the industry in Kolkata. In mid-2013, however, in recognition of the widespread problem of taxi refusal, the West Bengal government announced that it would launch a fleet of two thousand new cabs that would not refuse passengers. These vehicles would not be ambassadors; they would be sedan cars, compliant with Bharat Stage IV emission norms, and would provide not only dependable service but also physical comfort to passengers. As transport minister Madan Mitra is reported to have said, "We are trying to instill a new cab culture in the city. The vehicles will not only be modern, those driving these smart cabs will be forced to behave professionally. This way, tourists will get a better impression of the city." These taxis were painted blue and white, the city's theme colors under the Trinamool Congress party. The transformation that the move to the new cabs is intended to inaugurate is hence as much about improving infrastructure as about a desired change in the personality of the taxi driver, both of which are connected to the image of the city. The nature of the Bihari taxi driver's presence—his body, mannerisms, carriage, and speech—jars with the urban aesthetics desired by the urban middle class. The taxi drivers who are the subject of this book are operators of the older ambassador taxis, not the new entrants to the industry.

Although the overall rate of migration to Kolkata has declined in recent years, largely because of reduced employment opportunities following the closing of factories and local residents competing successfully against migrant workers (Mitra 2016), this trend appears to not apply to migrants from Bihar and Jharkhand, who continue to move to Kolkata to join the taxi trade; this is because driving the old yellow-black taxis remains unattractive to local youths in terms of both income and the nature of the labor. It is still unclear to what extent the coming of peer-to-peer ride-sharing technologies will recast migrant and local residents' attitudes toward transport work. There seems to be a preference for ride-sharing technologies among the middle classes because they are seen as "corporate" and hence more professional. Simultaneously, however, there is a rueful acknowledgment that drivers of application-based mobility service providers, in being dependent on navigation systems, are far from knowing city streets as well as drivers of the older yellow-black taxis.

Until the de-licensing of the passenger car industry in 1993, the domestically produced ambassador had a complete monopoly. Its brawny structure and design were deemed especially suitable to navigate the many potholes of Indian roads. As Nielsen and Wilhite (2017, 172) write, "The sturdy, stocky ambassador acquired a reputation as the quintessential Indian car, a symbol of Indian independence and modernity." The ambassador was the car of the political class and the social elite; most Indians could not afford it. For this reason, it is perhaps fitting that the majority of taxis in Kolkata were ambassadors, as taxis were similarly out of reach for most of the urban public. The car's elite status notwithstanding, the ambassador allowed a particular kind of relation to develop between the driver and the vehicle. As Sardar (2002, 212, cited in Hansen and Nielson 2017) explains, "The unchanging design of the Ambassador had allowed every mechanic of any ilk, every taxi driver to take it apart and put it together again blindfolded." This provided taxi drivers with a sense of autonomy and ownership over the vehicles they drove. Indeed, many of the operators of the ambassador taxi I spoke to relished their proficiency with handling the vehicle in case of a breakdown. Several of them said they feel safer in the ambassador than the lighter sedan cars that serve as Ubers and as no-refusal taxis. In 2014, however, ambassador production was discontinued. Unless production is resumed, ambassador taxis will disappear from the urban landscape in the years to come.

TRAFFIC POLICE

An early study of policing in India reveals that in cities about two-fifths of all men have had some personal encounter with the police. The vast majority of this contact is with traffic police (Bayley 1969). The cartographies of transport workers in the city emerge in relation to the regulatory presence of traffic policemen.

The Kolkata Traffic Police was established in 1874 with a total strength of seventeen men. This move was largely a direct response to strikes organized by palanquin bearers in the city. In 1973, the traffic department of Calcutta Police had about 945 personnel and seven patrol vans for traffic purposes (Chatterjee 1973). As of 2006, the traffic police force comprised about four thousand men. At present there are twenty-five traffic guards in the metropolitan area. Each guard is headed by two inspectors who are assisted by sergeants, head constables, constables, and home guards. Each police station also has a counseling center for women to handle issues ranging from street harassment to domestic violence. There are some seven hundred integrated CCTV cameras in major crossroads across the city, monitored in the traffic control room. The city has a total road length of 1,416.4 kilometers, which is the lowest among all major metro cities in the country. The Kolkata

Traffic Police force thus has a considerably difficult task in ensuring safe and efficient mobility in the city.

A Traffic Training School was set up in Kolkata in March 1953 with a view to impart required training to traffic personnel and also valuable civic education to the urban citizenry. In the main, the school provides a wide range of training programs for all ranks of the traffic department: inspectors, sergeants, constables, home guards, civic police volunteers, police drivers, and traffic wardens. These programs include both traffic education and the practical aspects of street administration such as CPR administration, disaster management, behavior training, and motor mechanism skills training. In recent years, there has been some investment in infrastructure development, with the school building now offering two small classrooms on the first floor and a larger room on the second floor, all fitted with air conditioners and LCD projectors. There also seems to be an awareness of the need to regularly update the curriculum in keeping with developments in modern traffic management techniques.

Workshops on safe driving practices targeted at bus, taxi, and auto drivers have been a crucial component of the school's activities in recent years. In 2014, some seventy taxi drivers participated in the workshops, and the number grew to nearly three thousand in 2015. For autorickshaw drivers, the figures were two thousand and three thousand in 2014 and 2015, respectively. This aspect of the Kolkata Traffic Police's endeavors received a huge stimulus when, in July 2016, the chief minister of West Bengal announced the launch of the Safe Drive Save Life campaign to reduce street accidents and improve the city's road culture. Between 1995 and 2000, accidents in Kolkata increased from 8,895 to 11,036, a 24 percent increase. In this period, the number of deaths from road accidents decreased from 480 to 452, a 5.8 percent decrease. However, in this same period the number of injuries caused by road accidents increased by 11 percent. According to police records, autorickshaw drivers received 4,124 and 4,023 official citations for rash driving in 2014 and 2015, respectively. The respective figures for taxis were 11,112 and 13,697. In 2015 some 200 cases of serious injury involving a taxi were registered, and 73 cases involved an auto. The Safe Drive Save Life campaign was envisioned as an intervention into this dismal state of safety on Kolkata's streets

A number of steps were planned toward this end. The introduction of stricter tests for driver's licenses and better training for would-be drivers were thought to be vital. The campaign has inaugurated a widespread effort at popularizing conversations on safe practices on city roads. Road safety messages and jingles are now played regularly on various radio stations, and banners and hoardings have been installed throughout the city. A series of public service advertisements have been produced and are screened on a regular basis at movie theaters across the city. These are also played at state government events. Furthermore, workshops are organized with schoolchildren to inculcate good road behavior from an early age.

The main aim of the Safe Drive Save Life campaign, however, is sensitizing transport workers to the pitfalls of reckless driving. The Kolkata traffic police have made concerted efforts to reach out to the unions representing autorickshaws, taxis, and buses to respond to the campaign. Sergeants and constables have personally urged transport workers they come into contact with to attend workshops, which are held daily in the various traffic guards of the city. The use of personal communication to dispense a public campaign signals the gendered character of the everyday state in Indian cities, an issue that I take up at length in later chapters. It is worth remembering that the Indian public generally, and working-class urban populations in particular, are deeply suspicious of the police, considering them to be rude, corrupt, and in collusion with criminals (Bayley 1969). Judging by the number of letters written to newspapers expressing this opinion, the urban middle class in West Bengal seems to be convinced that the traffic police force operates hand in glove with transport workers to sustain the welter of disorder that characterizes road life in Kolkata. The lives of the urban poor, on the other hand, provide ample evidence of the cunning of urban informalities that exposes them to the profoundly unsettling caprice of law and law enforcement officers. Perhaps in cognizance of this general suspicion toward the police, officers are being encouraged to forge more clear communication links with transport workers in the city. The Kolkata traffic police also organize the friendship club football tournament. This annual event enlists the participation of some four hundred neighborhood youth—all men—with the objective of establishing friendly relations between policemen and local youth. According to a report prepared by the state's Road Safety Council in August 2017, the number of road accidents in the region has been reduced by 19.52 percent since the adoption of these measures. Deaths and injuries on roads have also been reduced by 11.5 and 14 percent, respectively.

Conclusion

The overview of the transport scenario in Kolkata offered in this chapter provides a broad glimpse at the connections between public transportation and the social relations within which urban mobilities are embedded. A small but growing number of feminist studies are bringing analytical awareness to how women's urban lives are related to mobility opportunities in Indian cities. An ethnography of ride-sharing cabs in Hyderabad reveals that interactions between upwardly mobile women commuters and working-class male drivers are framed by mutual suspicion (Annavarapu 2022). A study from Chennai shows how the office taxi provided by IT companies to ferry women employees between home and work at night becomes a site of surveillance in which considerations about corporate budgets and safety are used to produce the figure of the respectable woman (Shakthi 2022). In the same city, a brand of scooters marketed to women is represented as safe and fun for young college-going women, who are protected not just from sexual violence but also from sexual intimacy with the wrong kind of men (Krishnan 2022).

Bearing these insights in mind, the following chapters move closer toward the lives of male transport workers and traffic police in Kolkata. Traveling along with these men as they traverse the different scales of the city, these chapters follow the shift in urban transport research away from techno-centric concerns to thinking about public transportation as a social field. As we proceed to unravel what these interactions on public transport tell us about men's relationship to urban life and mobility, we will encounter a range of urban characters coursing through the city. The first of these city characters is Kolkata's autorickshaw drivers.

2

Sociable Infrastructures

Autorickshaws

Sitting in the innermost seat of the autorickshaw in a south Kolkata neighborhood, waiting for the vehicle to fill up, my first co-passengers are an elderly middle-class woman and her very young granddaughter, returning from school. The young girl implores her guardian to let her have her own seat. Her grandmother glares in response, pointing at our auto driver by way of warning, and the young girl reluctantly makes space for other passengers who still haven't arrived. Just across this interior street—no more than a hundred meters in length—are a series of stores selling items ranging from cakes to electrical appliances, wrought-iron furniture, and women's undergarments. This side of the road, where we are waiting, lined by autorickshaws eager to quickly ferry as many customers as possible, is punctuated by a shabby public toilet and at least three tea stalls. One of these serves not just tea but also a full lunch menu and fried snacks for the evenings. Judging by the clientele who have gathered at this hour, their customers are mostly auto drivers and other working-class men. Today, a middle-aged man and his loudspeaker have taken a place on this pavement, and both are extolling the palliative powers of ointments laid out for sale on a mat in front of them. One tea merchant is amused and complains gently to no one in particular that this man's presence, so close to his shack, is hindering business. We have perhaps been waiting for five minutes when two young men—university students carrying long T-scales on their backs—approach the autorickshaw. One sits in front, next to the driver—himself not older than thirty years—while the other lodges himself on the back seat with us. We start off.

A corner of the windshield of the vehicle holds up a matchbox-sized poster of the Hindu goddess Kali. The dashboard carries small idols of Baba Lokenath (an eighteenth-century saint and mystic in the Indic region) and Ganesh (provider of prosperity and good fortune in Hindu religious mythology), and a plastic Indian flag. The loud drone of turning wheels, outdone suddenly by a bus honking furiously, stops for a while as the students alight in front of their university's gate. The elderly woman and her young companion adjust themselves away from me and sit a little more comfortably now that there is more room; she doesn't place the child on the one vacant seat next to her. At that time of day, the roads are not very busy, so the autorickshaw moves along slowly, hoping its languor will attract more passengers. Another autorickshaw, carrying its full quota of passengers, passes by our vehicle; this operator, recognizing our driver, slows down. As the two autorickshaws drive side by side, one driver asks the other about an athletic competition that is to take place that evening; our driver replies that he is eager to compete but hasn't played cricket in years and has completely lost his form. They also ask one another how far their passengers are traveling, to get a sense of business that working day. They nod at each other, and the other autorickshaw speeds ahead.

Soon a middle-aged, middle-class man hails our auto and proceeds to sit next to the driver. A young middle-class woman seats herself on the one vacant spot on the back seat. The two men begin talking about the worsening traffic in Kolkata and seem to agree that bus drivers, more than any other group, lack the required skill to navigate city roads properly. The young woman's mobile phone begins ringing, and we hear her assuring the caller that she will reach her destination on time.

Still on the call, she pulls out a hundred-rupee note to pay her fare and looks apologetically, and not without some consternation, at the driver for being unable to offer smaller change. The driver looks at her with displeasure but silently hands her the balance. After some time, the auto pulls over again and all the passengers, except me, disembark at a major crossroads. I am not alone for very long at all, as almost immediately a young working-class woman calls out and we stop to pick her up. As she sits next to the driver, I notice that he quickly adjusts his posture away from her. The auto doesn't instantly continue on its journey though, as the driver waits for more passengers. He leans out of the vehicle to his right, announcing his route's final destination to passersby. He glances at me and says, "I knew this spot would screw me over. No passengers here at this time ever, and the police bastards won't let us wait."

I take this chance to ask him a few questions. He is twenty-nine years old and has been a transport worker for seven years. He was previously employed as a floor staff member in a department store. I don't extend the conversation because I can see it is distracting him from identifying potential passengers. After a while, a lower-middle-class woman approaches; she has with her two young girls—one about ten years, the other about seven. The driver looks back inquisitively to ascertain how old the younger child is. The older girl takes the seat next to me, while the other girl sits on her mother's lap. The vehicle now packed to its permitted limit, we move speedily toward the end of the route.

In about ten minutes, we have reached our final destination and we all get off. As I am paying my fare, the driver begins, "Did you see how she brought such an old child all this way without offering to pay the fare? We notice all these things but turn a blind eye, and still we auto drivers get a bad name. No acknowledgment." The woman co-traveler, about whom this is being said, is still there and responds with great irritation, "My girl has had an accident, she has hurt her leg! If you wanted her fare why didn't you ask me? Why are you telling him [me] after I have paid? What kind of behavior is this?" As they argue, I wonder if I should wait or leave. After the woman has stomped off, the driver turns to me again, "You saw how she spoke? What good can one do to such people?"

This fieldwork vignette captures several of the themes of inquiry this chapter tracks. Public transportation, as a form of urban infrastructure, is a field of everyday interaction that mediates the gendered production of the urban social. City dwellers' assumptions about how infrastructures should work condition relations between people and hence the production of the urban itself in its ideational and built forms. The urban sketch hints at some of these competing and shared understandings of the proper usage of urban utilities, in this case public transportation. Clashes between the driver, who steers mobility, and the passenger, who must submit to this in some measure, provoke questions about agency in practices of movement and the politics of copresence in cities. This story concerning mobile forms of labor and the experiences of passengers is composed of quarrels and supportive gestures between passengers, among drivers, and with law enforcement officers. For autorickshaw drivers, passengers are a resource that they are competing for; but this competition also includes cooperation with one another: Drivers will not take passengers until the previous vehicle in the queue is full; when there are doubts about this, the errant driver is at pains to explain that he did no wrong. These narratives sit alongside frequent remarks from autorickshaw operators that this is a "competition market." This chapter adopts a micro-sociological approach to consider what interactions in the spaces of everyday commuting can contribute to understandings about the gendered character of urban infrastructures.

Public transportation systems operate not only as a physical link between different urban spaces but also as a zone of contact between diverse social groups in the city. The "throwntogetherness" (Massey 2005) of bodies and objects that characterizes cities is, therefore, acutely observable in the circuits of public transportation. Through ethnographic contact with the working lives of male autorickshaw drivers, the discussion that follows unravels the gendered politics of copresence in shared movement systems in the city. In doing so, it makes a feminist contribution to studies of urban infrastructures by revealing precisely how ideas of masculinity operate as an invisible structuring principle of mobility infrastructures in cities. Infrastructures often blend imperceptibly into the background of urban life, their workings invisible, especially to powerful social groups (Graham 2010). Similarly, masculinity—its hegemonic configurations, in particular—in being the assumed norm against which all else is judged, has historically escaped scrutiny. While there is now a vast body of scholarship that has separately explored the social relations in which urban infrastructures and masculinities are embedded, these two fields of inquiry have so far not been brought into dialogue with one another. Just as masculinities are formed simultaneously in large-scale institutions and face-to-face relationships (Connell 1996), so too do transport infrastructures operate as large-scale structures that yield socialities in the communicative contexts of shared travel (Bissell 2010). The ethnographic analyses of public transport bring into view the interface between cultures of masculinity and the social life of transport infrastructures in the everyday city.

The turn to infrastructure, in the social sciences generally but specifically in urban studies, has entailed conceptualizing provisioning systems not merely in terms of their functional capacities but also as having distinct social, spatial, political, and aesthetic effects (Graham and Marvin 2001; McFarlane and Rutherford 2008; Larkin 2013). A particularly insightful thread in this discussion has suggested that urban infrastructures make possible particular forms of sociality in cities and that a number of experiences of community, solidarity, and social friction are related to cities' material infrastructures (Rodgers and O'Neill 2012; Amin 2014). The experience of everyday life, it has been argued (Angelo and Hentschel 2015), involves repeated encounters with varied infrastructural systems, to the extent that the nature of city living can be partially narrated as a story of interactions with urban technological arrangements. If indeed infrastructures produce ideals of normality in the everyday city (Graham and McFarlane 2014), studies of urban infrastructures seldom consider the manner in which ideals of gender circulating in the urban public infuse encounters with infrastructural systems. In other words, urban scholars have not yet given sustained attention to how urban residents "do gender" in their everyday interactions with infrastructural arrangements in the city. Such a task would leaven critical urban theories, which, despite their keen awareness of social inequalities, seldom address issues of gendered power (Peake 2016). To this end, this chapter represents an initial foray into gendering extant knowledge of urban infrastructures through the lens of masculinity.

Conflict

In Kolkata, one order of conflict between drivers and passengers has to do with the autorickshaw being simultaneously a form of public transport and a privately owned vehicle. Drivers either own the vehicles themselves or, much more frequently, rent it from the owner. Some of the clash between drivers and passengers relates to the driver's demand that he be regarded as being in charge, even if he is not always the owner of the vehicle, and passengers' sense that autorickshaws are a public good, the use of which drivers merely facilitate. Everyday conflict around the proper way to inhabit the autorickshaw is rooted in drivers' awareness that business depends on the service being available to all those who can pay the fare and their desire that the private ownership/guardianship of the vehicle also be acknowledged by passengers. Most middle-class passengers, bolstered by a sense of class entitlement to public utility services in the city, are unwilling to accede to this latter demand and emphasize instead, in speech and behavior, the public character of the autorickshaw service. Such expressions of animosity between working-class men and middle-class passengers capture the link between the exercise of urban citizenship rights and male entitlement to property, a connection that might have intensified in a new cultural climate in India wherein commodity consumption is a key form of identity work and individual self-enterprise (Gooptu 2013b) is seen as the most rewarding way toward upward social mobility. Such contestations in the circuits of everyday commuting also bear witness to the urban middle class's willingness to participate in the privatization of public spaces in ways that expand their hold over the city, while taking recourse to a bourgeois notion of public good to reject the working poor's right to access public property. To the extent that gendered values often serve as an ideological ground on which class differentiations are enacted (Parry 2014), it is worth bearing in mind that cars have a specific relationship to ideals of masculinity; cars are seen variously as an extension of the male body or are feminized as objects to be forced into submission (McLean 2009). For the working-class urban male, without the means to purchase a private car, exercising such tenuous proprietorial control over a public transport vehicle becomes a form of enacting masculinity in the city.

For instance, drivers and passengers fall out all too often over the issue of the vehicle's speed. Complaints about reckless driving recurred in my interviews with passengers, even as auto operators alleged that passengers pressured them to drive fast to reach their destinations quickly. Conversely, the need to brake, especially when initiated by a passenger's sudden request, is often experienced as an affront by autorickshaw drivers, such that "being made to" slow down is experienced as having been aggressed upon, signaling the continuity that men forge between their bodies and the bodies of the vehicles they drive. Consider this field note: "As our autorickshaw is moving, another comes up next to us. The other driver, also in his early twenties, signals to this driver, making a zigzag motion with his hands, indicating that this driver doesn't know how to drive straight. This immediately sparks off a race on a long stretch of a major road, and lasts a good five minutes. The driver of the vehicle I am in 'loses' because a taxi emerging from an interior lane intercepts his passage."

Episodes such as this, which seriously compromise safety on city streets without any provocation from passengers, were far more common in the course of my ethnography than commuters urging drivers to drive fast. Indeed, while passengers are often impatient to get moving and, in the process, ignore the economic imperatives of the drivers to have a full complement of passengers, their demands seldom involve asking the driver to speed. On the contrary, several autorickshaw operators narrated with relish the thrill they derive from speeding:

> I like driving fast. Why? What can I do, the gear wants higher speed! Not that I drive in an insecure way. Smart driving, that's what I like. That means bypassing all this traffic cleverly, without touching any other vehicle or making your passengers feel uncomfortable. I love driving. It's like a video game for adults. All the vehicles around you are like different levels of difficulty in a video game. You have to find a way to evade all these obstructions and get ahead. I feel I am handling this tricky situation and moving ahead. It feels good. Though, I prefer driving a four-wheeler. Then I feel like Nicolas Cage!

There are now a number of studies conducted in Western contexts that explore men's use of cars to negotiate the demands of masculinity (Bengry-Howell 2005; Balkmar 2014). The two excerpts above—in particular the repeated references to tropes in contemporary visual and gaming cultures that valorize speed and racing—help us to identify the expressive possibilities of public transport infrastructures for the male driver as they relate to everyday life in the city. Interior lanes of neighborhoods in Indian cities are routinely used by male youth to play sports. The impromptu race between two auto drivers, by yoking speed with entertainment, captures how men's desire for leisurely pursuits may be displaced onto city spaces, wherein men collectively imagine and inhabit the city's main streets as a sporting ground. Scholars have argued that car cultures participate in the reproduction of traditional norms of masculinity with their emphasis on "competitiveness, freedom, mateship, display, technical skill and ability, speed and performance" (Walker, Butland, and Connell 2000, 157). Through the enactment of such forms of play with other men, male transport vehicle operators exercise a claim on a city that is perpetually recoiling from their reach, as a site of both labor and leisure. The second narrative accentuates the man's "embodied symbiosis with his machine" (Mellström 2004, 368) and establishes intentional risk taking—what this autorickshaw driver calls "smart driving"—as a psychological and behavioral strategy for men in coming to grips with the challenges of everyday life on the street. The imaginative reconstruction of road traffic as a video game allows the working-class transport vehicle operator to position himself as successfully maneuvering the pressures of urban life, wherein the different elements in the transport infrastructural landscape become metonyms for such vagaries of city living as the labor market, physical danger, law, interpersonal quarrels, and harsh weather.

Urban restructuring in India, especially in the postliberalization period, has proceeded by systematically reducing the visibility of the working poor while ensuring their availability to provide essential services to the middle classes. A large body of scholarship has outlined the spatial forms that such processes of marginalization take (Fernandes 2004; Donner 2012; Srivastava 2015). In this context it is useful to consider the ways in which social compulsions of masculinity inflect class contests around urban space and routines of everyday mobility in the city. The following field note captures spatial expressions of class relations between men in their encounters with urban transport infrastructures.

This autorickshaw driver was in his mid-twenties, his hair oiled abundantly and combed back, shirt and pants hanging loose on his thin frame. He was joking around with other drivers, as I waited inside his vehicle. Engrossed in the levity of the scene, I was surprised when an elderly middle-class man (over seventy years) hobbled toward the drivers to ask if this autorickshaw would go past Big Bazaar (a popular department store) and the young driver snapped at him in response: "You should have taken the auto going to Garia." The elderly man looked flustered and asked where he should go; he was told, grumpily, to sit in this vehicle. We started off when another man (about sixty years of age) and a woman aged about thirty years joined us in this autorickshaw. When we reached the department store, the driver alerted the elderly man; he, however, still looked lost and said that this was not the store he was looking for. He then mentioned Highland Park—which was in another direction— and that he was from New Delhi and was not familiar with Kolkata. The driver offered to drop him off at a point on his route that was closest to where this man wanted to go. I was struck by his helpful tone, in sharp contrast to his earlier irritable response. When we reached this crossroad, the driver again informed the man and, along with the other passengers, advised him on how to reach his destination. To my utter surprise the elderly man began to chastise the driver, saying, "You got a person unfamiliar with the city and you took him on a ride, didn't you?" Enraged, the driver reacted: "Did I ask you to take the wrong auto? Don't put the blame on me! This is why one should not help you people; I should have let you off at the wrong place itself!"

When Walter Benjamin (2006, 1) writes, in an oft-quoted passage, "Not to find one's way around a city does not mean much. But to lose one's way in a city, as one loses one's way in a forest, requires some schooling," he is clearly thinking of this urban experience as unmarked by gender. Benjamin's idea that enjoying being lost in the city needs some form of learning, however, is useful to sociologically understand gender differences in spatial ability. While the freedom to roam and relish the possibilities that being lost in the city can offer is a peculiarly male privilege (though curtailed by other vectors of social inequality), it is experienced by men as enjoyment only when they choose to be lost. While navigating the city in an intentional way, the ability to master urban space by knowing the physical characteristics of cities intimately is often a matter of masculine pride. In other words, being lost in the city can be experienced by men as loss of control and as a hurdle to accomplishing mastery of space (Srivastava 2010) as a prized index of masculinity. Control—and competition with those who threaten this sense of control—is a vital component of hegemonic masculinity, to the extent that situations in public spaces that lead to a loss of control generate fear in men (Day et al. 2003). If we now return to the scene described above, it becomes clear that the relative infirmity of old age, coupled with the vulnerability of being in an unfamiliar city and a middle-class suspicion of being deceived by working-class people, inclines the elderly man to think that he has been deliberately misled. This threatens his need to be in control of his spatial surroundings. When the older man alleges cheating, he is mistakenly reading public transport in terms of his experience in New Delhi. In Kolkata, autorickshaws do not run on a meter and have fixed fares. Therefore, while taxis in Kolkata may take longer routes to extract higher fares from unsuspecting passengers, the autos cannot do so because they follow designated routes on a shared basis. The younger man, on his part, reads this accusation as yet another instance of middle-class ingratitude to the working class and also as older men's tendency to wield authority over youth. It has been suggested that through micro interactions with/in urban infrastructure, urbanites interpret large-scale processes and read their situations in the wider social environment (Angelo and Hentschel 2015). The mundane conflict described here conveys how spatial imperatives of masculinity mediate men's competing sense of how transport infrastructures ought to be inhabited.

The working-class drivers of these vehicles often stage an affront to these forms of social control by trying to exert influence over the conduct of passengers in relation to the autorickshaw. Consider the course of this altercation between a forty-three-year-old auto driver and a middle-class woman in her fifties. He had asked her for change, which angered her tremendously.

Driver: "I asked you for change because where you will get off there is a lot of traffic, I need to let you off quickly and move on." The incensed woman responds: "You should just put up the fares on the windshield so that there is minimum talk required. You people don't realize the bad reputation you bring to Kolkata because of your behavior!"—Our driver becomes furious the moment the question of the city's reputation and auto drivers' behavior is raised—"You rich people have ruined the city for us and now you say it's because of us that the reputation of Kolkata is suffering?! All fault lies with us?!"

The production of urban middle-class identities in postliberalization India is connected to the collective will to remove poor people from public spaces of cities (Fernandes 2004). The altercation I witnessed suggests that the middle-class desire for "purification of space" (Sibley 1988) articulates itself also as a need to reduce interactions across classes even as they remain locked in unequal relations of exchange in the course of everyday urban living. In a postcolonial urban setting, such desires are complicated by particular ideas of progress and backwardness. Dominant social groups in the postcolonial city seek to diagnose and expunge "primitive" spaces and peoples from the modern metropolis (Srivastava 1998). In the moral ethos of contemporary urban India, while the person diagnosing "backwardness" in everyday urban encounters is inevitably middle class—that in this scene the accuser is a woman is surely incidental—the person whose behavior is connected to urban disrepute would always be not just working class but also male. The reason for this is that working-class men's labor in the city is visible in a way that working-class women's labor is not and hence gets written onto the image of the city more easily. Working-class women's labor, even when abundantly observable—such as in construction and building sites—frequently passes unnoticed. Moreover, a lot of women's labor is performed in the home, behind closed doors, or in enclosed spaces, such as at neighborhood bazaars. The desire for the respectable city, therefore, entails minimizing verbal contact with working-class men whose labor is visible in the city and necessary for its functioning but whose habits are despised. In this way mores of working-class male behavior, as they relate to public service provisioning, emerge as a key differentiating factor in the urban middle class's evaluations of urban reputation and intercity competition.

Critical approaches to the study of urban infrastructures emphasize the social relations between bodies and things that provisioning systems assemble. A feminist reading of infrastructure offers the important reminder that the body is always sexed and hence a locus of cultural norms of gender. This subsection of the chapter has integrated such a perspective into critical evaluations of urban infrastructures; it has done so by excavating the imprints of gendered power on infrastructural systems and the manner in which they mediate spatialized, class-based contestations between different social groups of men in the city.

Cooperation

It would, however, be a serious misrepresentation of urban interactions to suggest that hostility is predominant in all forms of copresence in shared transport services in cities. In many cities of the Global South, precisely because transport services cannot always be relied on to function as desired, urban actors must actively identify ways to make transport provisioning in the city work for them. This frequently requires collaborating with familiar strangers. In the course of my fieldwork in Kolkata, I regularly observed various forms of sociability between autorickshaw drivers and passengers, ranging from respectful greetings and banter to bawdy sexual humor, which indicated the need for urban scholars to heed mundane cooperation as we theorize copresence and shared use of urban infrastructures. Accordingly, the discussion of gestures of cooperation in this subsection follows the shift in infrastructure studies from an exclusive focus on physical structures to thinking about "people as infrastructures" (Simone 2004). Such an approach emphasizes the tenuous codes of collaboration between various urban actors that, through repetition, assume the form of infrastructural systems and hold together everyday urban living. The inherently protean character of cities makes urban living unpredictable. For this reason, inhabiting the city requires cultivating tacit knowledge of threat and whom one can rely on in times of crisis. In this section I demonstrate the distinctly spatial character of such collaborative improvisations by which urban dwellers function as infrastructures of support and the manner

in which these efforts are marked by ideologies of gender and masculinity.

When their vehicles are blighted by technical faults—such as a flat tire—drivers will stop an autorickshaw passing by to borrow its spare wheel. Indeed, a great proportion of passing conversations between autorickshaw drivers as they drive concerns vehicle maintenance, costs and procedures, and the traffic situation, which inhibits better business. At a traffic signal I once noticed an auto operator calling out to the adjacent driver, "Which company is your fan?" The other driver smiled and responded, "This isn't a fan; it's a Haier company air conditioner!" I had noticed the medium-sized cardboard piece tied to the railing of the adjacent autorickshaw, but it was this exchange that made me realize that it was intended as a makeshift fan, an effort at cooling on that extremely hot April day. The driver's seat is the warmest because it is close to the windshield and does not get any air. On another occasion, I noticed an autorickshaw slowing down to pick up a lost shoe from the road. The driver later explained to us, his passengers, that another driver on that route had misplaced his footwear and had asked other drivers to be on the lookout for it. Such experiments with infrastructure, which cohere into a shared vocabulary of understanding between autorickshaw operators, function as a communal resource to tide over the distresses—ranging from discomfort to danger—of transport labor in the city. Auto operators' understanding of the hardships of the city derive substantially from a collective sense that these are the peculiar burdens of working-class men in the city as they strive to provide for their families. For example, a recurring concern among autorickshaw drivers is road mishaps. Although road accidents may happen to anyone who steps outdoors, the far longer duration of time spent on city streets makes the likelihood of physical danger for transport workers particularly acute. Autorickshaw operators are aware that they are exposed to such urban dangers because they are poor men: they must earn money to sustain their families, and their employment options are severely limited. Therefore, they use the sociability and circumscribed geography of their trade to repose an element of confidence in each other. For public transport workers in the city, the abundant exposure to potentially hostile, even violent strangers generates a constant state of unpredictability. Collaborating with one another to forge a culture of the street by which they can expect some measure of reliability from each other becomes a crucial strategy to deal with the uncertain character of transport labor. Thus, when urban actors collaborate to manufacture an infrastructure of mutual reliance on city streets, they do so by exploiting the spatial possibilities of particular physical infrastructures in the city. Moreover, the provocation for such creative moves stems substantially from a shared recognition of their class and gender locations in the city.

Indeed, the city's potential for danger—even though it is variously conceived by different urban actors based on biography and social location—encapsulates both driver and passenger and becomes one of the bases for intersubjective understanding between them of the experience of moving through the city. I heard, for instance, an auto operator recounting to his passengers that a few days prior a woman in her forties, in her hurry to get to the metro station, had fallen down and hurt herself severely. Passengers then proceeded to participate in this recounting by offering their stories of accidents. Such anecdotal sharing of urban accidents recurred in interactions inside the autorickshaw. Anthropologists have studied the relation between narrative and healing to show how people's choices of narrative structure and rhetoric of expression are ways of emotionally processing difficult life circumstances (Mattingly 1998). Through collective storytelling, drivers and passengers together grapple with the physical hazards that everyday mobilities in the Indian city present. For instance, sometimes passengers use established narrative tropes to rein in a wayward driver: On one trip I heard a young woman passenger restrain a speeding driver by asking him cheekily, "Brother, have you been possessed by Superman?" leading to peals of laughter all around, as even the driver's face broke out in a smile. Here, the exaggerated heroic masculinity of a well-known fictional character is ironically invoked by a woman passenger to coax the male driver to adopt a safer mode of urban navigation. On another occasion, an older woman gently placed her hand on the shoulder of a young driver, who was honking furiously, and asked, "Why are you making so much noise unnecessarily, my child?" In this way, older women passengers may use a maternal vocabulary to chide unruly drivers, which operators may find acceptable.

It is worth emphasizing that the infrastructure of support that is forged by the sociable routine of autorickshaws as they move collectively along a familiar route includes within its folds passengers as well. One evening I saw a woman (mid-thirties, middle class) get inside an autorickshaw with two young children. The driver immediately asked a man sitting in the innermost seat of the vehicle to sit next to him instead. He explained to the male passenger that the woman and her children would be more comfortable if there was more air. I later asked this driver if he knew this woman; he replied that she was a familiar face, but nothing more, among the many passengers he ferries. Public familiarities of this sort may conditionally enhance women's experience of everyday commuting, though it is important not to overstate this since familiarity may just as well authorize moral policing. Nevertheless, most autorickshaw operators reported, with fondness, friendly relations with passengers. Passengers and drivers may share chewing tobacco, tea, or snacks, get to know each other as they wait for the vehicle to fill up and during commutes, even bring small gifts for one another. One young driver recalled an elderly middle-class woman passenger gifting him a small poster of a Hindu goddess with the blessing that it would bring him good fortune. The particular form of copresence that the autorickshaw enables opens avenues for conviviality between drivers and passengers. Simmel (1949) describes sociability—"association for its own sake"—as an ideal sociological world because in it every person's pleasure is dependent on the delight of others who are present. He characterizes it as a form of "play," as an "artificial world" because, in a sociable gathering, people must necessarily denude themselves of their individual material interests in order for the association to be pleasurable. For this reason, Simmel argues, sociability really works only within the same class strata and not across social divides. Consider this moment in an autorickshaw that I witnessed during my fieldwork:

The autorickshaw slows down near a Montessori school, in front of which several women are waiting with toddlers; school is clearly over for the day. A woman in her early thirties boards the auto with her daughter. The woman continues speaking loudly to her daughter, cooing baby talk, asking the child why she has cried all day in school. The child affirms reluctantly that indeed she wept the entire day. This chatter generates a great deal of amused interest among the driver and passengers (a middle-class woman in her late fifties, and lower-middle-class man in his early forties) and they join in the conversation. The driver asks the child affectionately, "What will happen if you cry like this every day in school, tell me?" Everyone in the auto is smiling and the atmosphere in the vehicle is one of affectionate banter.

In a while, as the older woman gets off the vehicle and the other woman makes way for her, the male passenger holds on to the child to help her mother.

Simone (2008, 76) has directed attention to the "egalitarian ethos" that emerges when residents recognize their immersion in a common urban field and invest in forms of collaboration for mutual benefit in ways that subordinate rationales of social hierarchy. The scene described above distills one such artificial moment produced by the social life of transport infrastructure, which momentarily suspends class differentiations in the city. Such fleeting contact with strangers creates opportunities for the urbanite to temporarily dissolve the isolation of urban commuting and the inherent unpredictability of urban life in the company of friendly strangers. It is noteworthy, however, that the spontaneous joy of association between biographical strangers that the scene captures is facilitated by the respectability of young middle-class motherhood in the city at a respectable hour of the day. Indeed, the gestures of cooperation between male drivers and women commuters, which this discussion has documented, depend on a familial ideology of gender. Thus, when a woman restrains a rash driver, she does so by addressing him as her younger brother; when an older woman blesses a driver, she establishes with him a filial relation; when the driver assuages the discomfort of a woman traveling with her young children, he recognizes her social role as a mother. These instances demonstrate the extent to which normative values of the public and intimate spheres structure everyday interactions in/with infrastructures in the city. The infrastructures of support through which men and women make shared movement systems viable for them rest on patriarchal valuations of the public-private divide. The public life of urban infrastructures is, therefore, better understood when considered in relation to the private, especially in Indian cities where neighborhoods create social interiors in public spaces through a range of everyday practices that provisionally domesticate the urban social.

Such forms of conviviality, set alongside querulous episodes on city streets, draw attention to the constitutive part played by the joy of everyday sociabilities and unremarked gestures of support in the maintenance of the urban social fabric. The conviviality of sociable infrastructures of shared mobility simultaneously index how male privilege in the city is maintained and how the marginalized make urban space hospitable for themselves. The following segment continues this line of inquiry by focusing on erotic encounters in the routines of urban commuting.

Sexual Encounters

In a well-known scene in Rituparno Ghosh's 1997 film *Dahan* (Crossfire), a group of men accost a young, newly married woman as she is waiting on a poorly lit Kolkata street, looking for a ride home. As the men harass her, an autorickshaw carrying two men and a woman approaches. The woman sitting inside the auto—a schoolteacher we later learn—notices the scene that is unfolding nearby and yells out to the men to stop troubling the distraught woman. She urges the driver to get closer to them; he refuses, saying he does not wish to get involved. Disgusted with their apathy, the woman decides to get off the vehicle and go help, even as her male co-passengers advise her against it.

Quite unlike this portrayal of indifference, almost all the transport workers I spoke to displayed a keen awareness of the ways in which sexual harassment of women plays out in public spaces, particularly inside the autorickshaw. Their narratives reveal alertness to the strategies women use to manufacture safety in the outdoors and some of the provocations for men's empathetic reactions to street harassment faced by women. A forty-eight-year-old driver told me,

> There are some passengers, mostly older men, who irritate women in the auto. We can see clearly what they do. Most women know how to deal with such situations. Some speak up,

some are too scared to raise objections. Then there are other women who immediately sit beside the driver. This is because the auto driver is traceable, the passengers are not. If there is any trouble it will be from one person who is identifiable. [Do you say anything when you notice these things happening?] If the woman does not object it is not right for us to say anything. But if the women raises objection then we chime in and say, "Please sit properly." Passengers say, "No I haven't done anything." If you haven't done anything why is the woman complaining, she is not mad!

Far from the victim blaming that pervades reactions to instances of sexual harm, the drivers I interacted with expressed a willingness to believe women's allegations of harassment and not men's defenses. Their reasons for this range from recognizing that lack of safety will dissuade women from using the auto and hence impede business to recognizing harassment as a moral wrong. Thus, if this driver waits for women to register protest before reacting to an instance of harassment, other drivers told me that they intervene the moment they notice inappropriate touching. A thirty-two-year-old driver recounts: "If you travel on the same route every day you notice things. Passengers become familiar. I know this middle-aged man, a government employee. His wife and daughter are both very good looking; the daughter is married. He always waits to see if there is an attractive woman in the auto already, only then does he get up. Twelve months of the year, through the seasons, he wears a half-shirt. One day I confronted him. After that he avoids taking my auto. I also told other drivers to watch out for him."

The particular mode of operation of Kolkata autorickshaws, which travel fixed routes, enables the creation of an infrastructure of support for women commuters. Drivers come to know where some of their regular passengers stay, who their family members are, and what professions they are in. This passing familiarity between drivers and commuters, facilitated by the social life of the autorickshaw, fosters a field of interaction in which drivers feel encouraged to intervene in encounters involving harassment as well as visually police men who are seen as likely to inflict such harm. Thus, over time, drivers come to remember male passengers who have a habit of harassing women co-passengers and refuse to accept their business; they even create a culture of shaming the perpetrator. "There is this one man, fifty-odd years, who waits around like a greedy dog for a young woman with a developed figure. These faces I remember and never take them in my vehicle. Some of these passengers are unable to make eye contact with me because they know that I know."

One thirty-eight-year-old driver goes so far as to keep a stick handy in the vehicle to intimidate habitual offenders and recalls compelling a younger man to hold his ears and apologize to the woman he had harassed. Most drivers also readily acknowledge that on occasion such harassment ensues from autorickshaw operators themselves: "There are some drivers too whose left arm is diseased. I ask them too: brother, is your left elbow alright? I'm sure they don't leave any women, so when my mother or wife gets on they must also face such things from them?"

Significantly, the cramped architecture of the autorickshaw notwithstanding, drivers admitted no doubt in understanding which forms of physical contact constitute harassment. As the narratives documented here show, the recognition of street harassment of women as harm, and hence as morally reprehensible, is premised both on profeminist ideas of consent as well as on patriarchal understanding of women's bodies as belonging to the husband/father. In my discussions with drivers about precisely what about sexual harassment makes it seem "wrong" to them, it was not unusual to hear the same man say that it is wrong because the woman has not agreed to such physical contact as well as because she is someone's sister/daughter/wife and therefore needs to be given due respect. Thus, the infrastructure of support that I am identifying as made possible by repeated encounters between the same driver and passengers follows simultaneously the logic of male protectionism and ideas about women's right to refuse sexual advances from unfamiliar men. The recognition that some auto drivers are also sex offenders, however, often accompanies allegations of unfair blame that is collectively felt to be meted out to this professional group. I heard many operators reiterate that "society" uses these few "bad" men as examples to defame all autorickshaw drivers. One kind of strategic reaction to this disrepute, as the opening vignette of this chapter demonstrates, entails drivers developing elaborate bodily gestures that mark physical distance from women passengers.

It is worth emphasizing that inasmuch as cities are ubiquitously sexualized, the social life of the autorickshaw includes not only street harassment but also erotic exchanges ranging from the flirtatious to the sexual. The fleeting familiarity between working-class men (drivers) and middle-class women (passengers), forged in the course of their daily travels, often affords opportunities for banter that would otherwise be rare between these two social groups. Consider the following field observation: "A driver in his late twenties tells a middle-class woman (also in her twenties) who has just gotten off the auto and is paying her fare, 'Please give me change, if no one gives me change I will have to commit suicide!' They both realize the sheer exaggeration of his words and burst out laughing together. The woman gives him change and he drives off."

Occasionally, some of these interactions become flirtatious and may even lead to sexual/romantic relations, though none such encounter narrated to me crossed boundaries of class. A twenty-eight-year-old driver told me, "In this profession, many times we come across girls who are flirty. They come sit next to the driver, talk in a sexy way, give us their phone numbers. Some drivers wait for particular girls they like, they keep track of their schedule, pick them up, drop them off. I know some drivers who have had affairs with girls they met in the auto."

These girls are mostly working- and lower-middle-class women, employed in beauty parlors, in cosmetic shops, or as salespersons. Some drivers—mostly younger, unmarried men, but several older, married men as well—reported renting rooms to have sex with women whom they met first as passengers. I was told that a few of these encounters led to marriage.

City of Fear

Feminists have largely assumed that cisgender, heterosexual men are strangers to feelings of fear in the city (Pilot and Prabhu 2012). As Rachael Pain (2000) points out, spatial aspects of men's fear in the city have hardly been considered in a sustained way within feminist urban studies. The narratives of urban living that I elicited from my respondents demonstrated the manner in which men's fear of crime in the city manifests itself in spatial terms. Men's conceptions of urban danger also question footlooseness as an enviable value of masculinity. Many auto operators I spoke to articulated, on the contrary, a desire for spatial rootedness, explicitly related to the management of dangers posed by everyday mobilities in the city. To a large extent, this emphasis on spatial familiarity conditioned their choice of profession within the domain of transport work. Autorickshaw drivers expressed, for example, a clear preference for the auto in comparison to driving a taxi in Kolkata. Repeatedly, the reason cited for this choice was that the taxi takes the driver to far-off places where he knows no one to ask for help in times of need. The prospect of moving away from known territory was accompanied by apprehensions of discomfort of different levels, from mere inconvenience through physical danger to death. "I picked this route among other auto routes because this area is familiar to me. This is my locality, everyone knows me here. If I am in an accident or my vehicle breaks down, people here will recognize me and come forward to help. Park Circus is Hindi, they won't help me. With taxis, you have no control over where you are and when. If I run into any trouble somewhere far, no one will come forward to support me. It's much easier being in a known locality."

While this thirty-eight-year-old auto driver articulated the question of safety in the city in terms of ease and convenience, thereby avoiding a language of fear, other men expressed unequivocally a calculus of spatial danger in the city. Another auto driver, thirty-two years of age, who drove a taxi for a year before giving it up, remembers,

It was late evening, a Muslim woman got on with two children, asked me to take her to Beckbagan (a predominantly Muslim neighborhood). When I dropped her the meter read twenty-five rupees. She said she would be back and disappeared for half an hour into a house. She sent back a man with the money, but by that time she owed me forty rupees. He started fighting with me about this; soon enough young men in the locality came up and started threatening me. Alone, I could not do anything. If they hit me, slap me, I would not be able to defend myself. I didn't know anyone there. So whatever money he offered, I took and came away. But I was so angry that I just parked my car in a corner, tied a cloth around the meter and sat there fuming for two hours. Whoever came up to me, I refused. Then I realized I have to pay the car owner at the end of the day and started accepting passengers again.

A forty-three-year-old man who has worked as an auto driver for two decades also used to drive a taxi before he joined the auto trade. He encountered a number of problems in that profession and, unable to resolve them, decided to make the switch. A particular incident triggered this decision:

One day, I took a passenger in Metiaburuz [a lower-middle-class Muslim neighborhood]. You know how some roads have many speed breakers in a short distance? I had to drive slowly. The passenger, a young Muslim man, put a knife to my throat and said, "You have taken out a taxi, drive it like a rocket." He used such abusive language I cannot repeat. I kept my cool, asked him to take another cab as I was feeling unwell. After that I went straight to the owner, returned the car, and that very day gave up the taxi trade.

To make sense of these narratives it would be important to remember that while Kolkata did indeed witness communal riots during the Partition of India, in the seven decades since, unlike in many other Indian cities, there has been no large-scale violence in this city between Muslims and Hindus. The concentration of class-based disparities has made it much more difficult to incite communal violence in Kolkata, and religious minorities have had access to an everyday sense of security not found in other cities in the country (Sen 2008), although this security is speedily waning with the spread of right-wing Hindu ideology in the region. Widespread anti-Muslim cultural prejudice of the Hindu middle classes in addition to memories of communal violence have resulted in sequestered enclaves of dwelling for Muslims in Kolkata since the 1950s (Chatterjee 2015). The emergence of Muslim-majority neighborhoods in Indian cities has been read by scholars as an effort by the community to produce safety through residential clustering (Gayer and Jaffrelot 2012). If, as Blom Hansen (1999) has suggested, the coexistence of Hindus and Muslims in Indian cities is characterized by "back-to-back intimacy" that proceeds through mutual misrecognitions and suspicions, the narratives of public transport workers convey the extent to which such apprehensions configure men's relationship to other men by taking distinctly spatial forms. Experiences of physical threat and humiliation stoke the dominant Hindu imagination of Muslim-majority neighborhoods as spaces of lawlessness and violence and the Muslim male as inherently aggressive; they also outline geographies of male fear through which, at least Hindu men, inhabit urban spaces. Men's feelings of fearfulness in the city, therefore, are also articulated in spatial terms and necessitate strategies of avoidance through which a sense of security in public spaces can be produced. Such experiences and imaginations of urban life construe the outdoors as always potentially dangerous and the world of strangers as largely indifferent, if not overtly hostile, to the lone male visitor.

I witnessed firsthand the actualization of apprehensions of danger and the structures of mutual support that autorickshaw drivers depend on as they navigate city streets. In the middle of one of my ride-along interviews with a twenty-eight-year-old auto operator, we noticed a sizeable crowd surrounding an autorickshaw parked on the pavement; several other autorickshaws were also parked nearby. The driver of the vehicle I was in immediately stopped, and we both got off to see what had happened. We were told that a woman had darted onto the road and this autorickshaw had swerved to the left to avoid a collision, flipping over in the process. The driver looked shaken and complained that his chest hurt. It quickly became apparent that most of the men who were surrounding him were auto drivers. The driver of the vehicle I was in removed a bottle from his vehicle and offered this driver some water. There was a hint of exaggeration in this gesture of kindness, aware as he was that I was watching. Some drivers offered to take the injured driver to a hospital, but the man insisted that he would be fine with a little rest. As we continued on our journey, the driver shared with me the story of how a friend of his, an auto driver, had died instantly after his ribcage was smashed by a truck as it sped out of control down an overpass. When the interview ended and I was taking my leave, he told me with a wry smile, "We take Allah's name and leave in the morning but we don't know if we will return in the evening."

What is noteworthy in this otherwise unremarkable accident scene in urban India are the community ties that bind autorickshaw drivers as they navigate everyday difficulties on city streets. Although accidents may happen to anyone who steps outdoors, their time spent on city streets increases the likelihood of physical danger for transport workers. This awareness among auto operators forges a sense of belonging to a professional group, with its accompanying promise of mutual support, devoid of which the city is experienced as a threatening place. In this way, autorickshaw drivers use the sociability and circumscribed spatial routine of their trade to establish a "trust culture" (Sztompka 1999) through which they can repose confidence in each other. Sztompka understands trust to have two main elements: belief and commitment. Trusting people entails that we believe that they will behave in ways that we expect them to. It also entails the obligation to reciprocally offer the kind of behavior that others owe us in a trust culture. For public transport workers in the city, the abundant exposure to strangers generates a constant state of unpredictability. Collaborating with one another to forge a trust culture in which they can realistically expect some measure of reliability from each other becomes a crucial strategy to deal with the uncertain character of transport labor.

It is also worth emphasizing that some of the threat that these men expressed, as being part of their inhabitation of the outdoors, relates to not just physical harm but also the pitfalls of becoming emotionally unsettled on the road: "If a passenger behaves badly and I get worked up early in the morning, I still have to work the entire day. They will go away but I will remain angry and it will keep me from working well. What will my family eat, how will my children go to school?" For these men, care of the self, itself connected to the male provider role and familial duty, informs a pragmatics of handling everyday conflict in the city. Apprehensions of such conflict, of varying orders of severity, stem from both the gender and class positions of auto operators. In other words, transport workers' vulnerability to and management of the particular problems they encounter in the city are to be explained by their social location as working class and as men. Several auto drivers shared the opinion that their economic situation would improve significantly if the autorickshaw were metered, as in other Tier 1 Indian cities. And yet this same group of drivers was eager to emphasize that they did not want access to the city at large, like taxis. Instead, they wanted metered autorickshaws to be zoned, with freedom of movement within that demarcated area only. Such collective desires connote men's negotiation of the imperative of breadwinning with their sense of spatial danger and comfort in the city. If we conceptualize apprehensions of failure as a form of threat to the sense of self, we may read in these desires a will to produce ontological security for the male self by fulfilling expectations of masculinity and guarding against danger to the body by collectively producing structures of community support in the city.

Fear in the city for working-class men thus has a variety of meanings that vary with their location in other social groups. Based on my fieldwork, fear seems to encompass apprehensions of physical violence and humiliation from other men, of road accidents, of the breakdown of infrastructure they are responsible for, of law enforcement. These fears are all part of the urban danger that envelops city people generally, if in different ways. Who, after all, doesn't fear stranger violence and the hazards of street accidents? Sally Engle Merry (1983) theorizes this general urban danger as a feeling of vulnerability impelled by encounters with strangers who are seen as likely to turn hostile. A large body of scholarship has demonstrated the cultural link between masculinity and the willingness to use varying degrees and forms of violence to establish status (Messerschmidt 1993; Kimmel and Mahler 2003; Whitehead 2005). Thinking about urban danger using the lens of masculinity suggests that, as gendered subjects, men's fears in the city are tied to the dread of failing to dislodge the provider role and the feminization of being unable to defend oneself from physical harm. The city becomes a site of fear for men when it forces them into situations in which they find themselves unequal to actualizing traditional definitions of maleness.

Disappointment and Disrespect

Much of the recent scholarship on working-class masculinities has delved into the impact that neoliberalism has had on men's lives. These studies (Cornwall, Karioris, and Lindisfarne 2016; Walker and Roberts 2018) reveal that the shift from an industrial to a service economy, where work is often precarious, has largely undermined poor men's capacity to fulfil the traditional expectations of masculinity, in particular the ability to provide. The ethnographic literature on working-class masculinities in India, as they relate to cultures of work and family life (Chopra 2003; Chopra, Osella, and Osella 2004; Jeffrey, Jeffery, and Jeffery 2008), has traced the complex links between masculine identity, respectability, and financial security. Autorickshaw drivers' inhabitation of the city is framed by a collective sense of being disrespected. Indeed, it is this sense of disregard that levels auto operators' varied everyday experiences of the city, despite their location in other vectors of social inequality. "Most people see the auto profession in very poor light. Passengers abuse us. Police are after us. Auto drivers are blamed for everything. Pedestrians are never fined for the way they walk. The newspapers television channels—Bengali, English all—constantly carry reports of us having committed some wrong or the other" (forty-three-year-old driver).

In addition to abusive passengers and police threats, auto drivers also grapple with the contempt drivers of other vehicles show them. The collective feeling that auto drivers will be blamed for every untoward situation on city streets creates a reluctance among them to intervene in situations that demand the help of strangers, such as accidents. The two autorickshaw bays at the ends of each route have the capacity to park thirty vehicles each, whereas there are typically six hundred vehicles on busy routes. Operators thus have to be on the move continuously. They resent this compulsion and connect their inability to lay spatial claims on the outdoors to the general disrespect meted out to poor people in the city. Eschewing the tendency to couple working-class masculinity solely with dominant values of gender, some recent studies have identified varieties of male identity projects within this class formation that may be more egalitarian (Roberts 2013). Many autorickshaw drivers I spoke to recognized that the desire to be respected involves according similar respect to other forms of labor that are stigmatized. A twenty-eight-year-old auto operator reasoned, for instance, that there is nothing wrong with women who offer sex for pay because "we are all working to feed our stomachs." Thus, if precarious employment strengthens traditional gender beliefs in men, in some instances it also creates conditions for them to repudiate disrespectful attitudes toward gendered forms of labor.

Everyday expressions of disrespect toward their lot are handled by auto operators in various ways. Some of the younger drivers harbor aspirations of moving out of the transport industry to drive luminaries in private cars, start small businesses, or even undertake office work because these are respectable professions. "I only want to earn more money. From a young age I realize people will only respect you if you have money. So I was never really interested in studies. If I have money I can look after my family much better. I will buy a good house, my family will live in comfort.

I want to get ahead because no one respects the poor" (twenty-eight-year-old driver).

Such yearnings are curtailed, however, by their assessment of what the city makes possible for men of their social position. Most realize that they may never be able to make the switch to a more rewarding career. Perhaps as a reaction to such disempowering assessments of their situations, some drivers characterize transport work as affording, despite the poor monetary benefits, more freedom than a regular office job. Given the unavailability of practical alternatives, often the only ways around everyday indignities are discursive ones. Some operators claim that the social standing of passengers has no meaning for them. Passengers are estimated simply in terms of the fares they pay, and this is made clear to particularly uncivil commuters who use their privilege to insult auto operators. Drivers also stressed that if you are born in a poor family, you have no option but to endure (*bardasht*) hardships. I asked a thirty-eight-year-old auto operator what his dreams were as a child. He went quiet for a while before telling me that he had several dreams but that there was no point in thinking about them now. I urged him to share what was on his mind: "I wanted to study more. Thought if I get a degree I will be able to provide better for my family. My sisters will also be able to get an education and do well for themselves. But that hasn't happened."

Nandini Gooptu (2013b) has identified the emergence of a new enterprise culture in India, "the creation of new Indians, whose dreams, passions, and desires fuel and propel all else, and whose powerful, newly liberated, capacity to aspire is in itself an asset." Indeed, the city as a space of "aspirations" (Appadurai 2004), "passions" (Amin and Thrift 2002), and "potentialities" (Simone 2016) has received much attention from urban scholars. The narratives of transport workers documented here invite attention to the obverse of urban aspiration, that is, the city as a crucible of disappointment. In my exchanges with transport workers, I was struck by the number of operators who stressed that the city of Kolkata had not changed substantially over the years: "The city has remained the same since I was small. Yes, roads have improved, overpasses have been built, there are much more private cars, living here has become more expensive. But nothing much has changed for me" (forty-three-year-old driver).

Unemployed young men's lives in India, it has been suggested, embody a particular relationship to time. Being young, male, and jobless lead to the cultivation of a habit of waiting, of finding ways to bide time and dwell in this state of limbo (Jeffrey 2010). The reactions of transport workers that emphasize the city's changelessness even in the face of rapid urban development capture another kind of entanglement between time and space in the production of masculinities. In bearing witness to the changing infrastructural landscape of the city that only reproduces the conditions of their marginality, working-class men organize their identity in relation to both time and space. Many young auto drivers reported that their fathers had been operators too during their working days and that they did not see any qualitative improvement in their lives through this generational shift. Much of their fathers' difficulties to earn and provide sufficiently for their families remained their struggle as well. That the question of urban change was read by transport workers through the lens of their roles within the family as providers demonstrates the extent to which the ideology of breadwinning mediates men's relationship to the city. Many auto operators told me that they want "passengers who will cooperate, who will have a sense that we are someone's father, someone's husband, someone's son, that our families need to eat and our children need to go to school." The quest for respect in the city is therefore tied to the quest for respect within the family, itself impelled by the identification of masculinity with providing. For working-class men, therefore, the city as a crucible of disappointment indexes their struggle against the failure to approximate the male social role. A thirty-four-year-old autorickshaw operator explained his dilemma in response to my question of whether it would ease the financial burden on him if his wife also earned, "You see, no woman in my family has ever worked. My mother has not worked. The wives of my elder brother don't work. But it's true that expenses have gone up so much in the past few years that it would be good if my wife worked as well. But I hesitate to ask her. I feel a sense of shame. As if I have failed in my duty. So I don't ask. I would rather endure the cruelty [*zulm*] this city throws at me."

Conclusion

The "new" approach to infrastructure, as we have seen, is distinguished by its emphasis on the social life of urban provisioning systems and the complex sociabilities they enable. The diagnosis of the social character of infrastructures has been an important conceptual addition to urban studies. This has entailed, in part, a turn to the everydayness of infrastructures in the city and the diverse effects that the encounters of urbanites with infrastructural arrangements generate (Graham and McFarlane 2014). The discussion in this chapter conceptualized public transportation in cities as a social field where rituals of urban inhabitation are learned and performed as specifically gendered acts. It identified the various compulsions of masculinity that charge transport infrastructures with hostilities that override norms of urban civility as well as augment sociable copresence between and among genders in cities. The revelation of transport infrastructures in the city as enmeshed with different configurations of masculinity opens up urban infrastructure studies to feminist insights. If critical urban theory has recuperated urban infrastructural systems from the cloak of invisibility, this chapter has shed light on the invisible regimes of masculinity through which infrastructures mediate the interactional order of the everyday city.

The ethnographic vignettes reported in this chapter suggest two kinds of entanglement between working-class masculinity and urban infrastructures. On the one hand, physical infrastructures of the city largely emblematize poor men's frustrated ambitions and operate as a conduit of gendered conflict with the urban middle class and women who are perceived to be upwardly mobile. On the other hand, the associational life of transport systems generates social infrastructures that enable them to collaborate with other urban actors, provisionally produce a web of reciprocal support, and manage fears of unfamiliar spaces. Transport workers make creative use of the autorickshaw's routines of sociability to generate a provisional architecture of cooperation that makes the everyday city hospitable for them. Thus, the urban infrastructural landscape exercises a dual pull on the gendered subjectivities of poor men in the city. Even as urban infrastructures are experienced by working-class men as a reminder of the disrespect meted out to them regularly and their struggle to accomplish the norm of respectable breadwinner masculinity, these infrastructures also function as a terrain that allows other expressions of masculinity—such as risk taking, mastery over space, male camaraderie, and protectionism toward women—to be enacted and affirmed. In this, the urban poor's encounters with infrastructure also convey their effort to find a semblance of joy in everyday living, while fighting to survive in the city. Furthermore, by establishing quasi-familial ties with other drivers and passengers, transport workers forge a tenuous sense of community and reliability amid the unpredictability of urban life. While certain physical elements in the city's infrastructural landscape come to represent structural constraints on working-class masculinity—especially breadwinning and the respect that accompanies it—the social life of mobility infrastructures is seized by these men to develop other competencies of masculinity that allow them to inhabit the city with a measure of confidence. In these ways, cultural logics of masculinity infuse everyday encounters with urban infrastructural systems.

Everyday mobilities in the city are produced by social processes that operate at different spatial scales. In other words, the movement of objects and people through which the quotidian city comes into being are mediated by relationships to localities both near and afar. While this chapter has considered the co-constitution of masculinity and urban space by focusing on the circumscribed geography of autorickshaws as they traverse designated routes, the following chapter moves this discussion from the scale of particular neighborhoods to the city at large. As we alight from the autorickshaw and take a taxi, we find ourselves in the midst of a city that is very different from the one we have witnessed so far.

3

Unaccustomed Streets

Taxis

They approached in a group. A few young men. Two in frayed jeans and T-shirts, two more in worn-out pants and shirts. Me and two others from my village were waiting near a bus stop; we were all in taxi drivers' uniforms. One of them asked us, "Where is your taxi, we need to go." We replied that we are off duty, it is past eleven at night; they would find taxis at the major crossroad nearby. The boys immediately started abusing us: "You are wearing uniforms why won't you go? Biharis are like this, Biharis are like that!" We reacted and they began throwing punches at us. Soon other local boys joined them and beat us up. We could not do anything, we had to run away. We immediately went to our boss's place; he is Bengali. We took refuge in his place for a while. Then, when we went out to go home, we saw they were waiting for us, some thirty of them. They beat us up again. We had some 1,400 rupees; they snatched that money from us. Our vehicle owner is an influential person in the area. He asked us to lodge an FIR, and he followed it up with the local politician. He promised us that this won't happen again. That's how the situation ended. We were beaten up because we are from outside. They would not dare beat up a Bengali driver so easily. We are easy targets because we are alone here.

The experience of moving away from familiar places is always meaningful. The journey from village to city, in search of employment, certainly means different things for different men; but the general significance of this shift in the lives of migrant taxi drivers is perhaps demonstrated by the vivid clarity with which they recall their initial days in the city. Ram Prasad's narrative of arrival in Kolkata in the early 1980s—he hails from Samastipur district in Bihar and is now fifty-eight years old—countervails the hackneyed tropes through which the villager's early impressions of the metropolis are often depicted. Far from registering any sense of wonderment at the sheer size of the city, its cacophonous soundscape, its heterogeneous crowds, its glamour, the eighteen-year-old Ram's first impressions of Kolkata were most underwhelming: "So *this* is what a city is? The buildings look run down and there is so much dirt everywhere!" Like most migrant taxi drivers, Ram spent his first few months in Kolkata trying to learn the city. On being asked to recall these early days, many drivers emphasized the pleasures of roaming an unfamiliar land—itself a male privilege—through streets that would, over the years, become familiar. Several hours of these initial days followed the trails of eager feet, keen to explore unaccustomed streets, pausing only briefly for a quick meal in roadside food stalls and in city parks for an afternoon snooze. The social contacts through which they came to the city—typically an uncle, an older cousin or brother, or some other kin-like figure from the village community, who had found employment in the city and knew its ways—would mostly encourage this temporary release from the demands of work life; if these young men were to be taxi drivers in Kolkata, it was important to first gather a feel of the city, a working familiarity with its roads. These older men—variously employed as taxi drivers themselves or as car mechanics, construction workers, or neighborhood grocery store owners/workers—to whom both the village and the city were well known, gradually initiated these younger men into the transport industry: teaching them how to drive, procure a driver's license, and find a vehicle in need of a driver and the tasks involved in maintaining the vehicle and related paperwork.

Bihar, a state in eastern India, contiguous with West Bengal, Uttar Pradesh, Jharkhand, and Nepal, has a long history of out-migration, traceable to the nineteenth century, a time when the region provided indentured laborers to British colonies such as Fiji and the West Indies as well as to the jute mills of Bengal (Priyadarshini 2014). Economic underdevelopment and slow industrialization have kept the economy of Bihar, despite being a mineral-rich state, dependent on agriculture and migration (Jha and Pushpendra 2014). Since the 1970s, low wages and meager prospects of gainful employment in Bihar have impelled vast numbers of men to migrate to the relatively affluent region of central Bihar, but mostly to states like West Bengal, Haryana, Punjab, and Maharashtra, to work as transport vehicle drivers, watchmen, barbers, washermen, sweepers, and construction workers (A. K. Roy 2011). A majority of male migrants from rural Bihar in Kolkata live in slum settlements in the city, and areas such as Cossipore and Howrah have a predominantly Bihari population (Mukherjee 2009). Most migrant taxi drivers in Kolkata return to their homes in Bihar at least once in a year, staying between fifteen and sixty days. They plan their visits usually to coincide with the harvesting seasons and important religious festivals in the region. This pattern of migration and the proximity of Bihar to Kolkata allow migrant men who come to the city to work as taxi drivers to retain intimate connections to their villages. The maintenance of such ties enables them to grapple with the insecurity of working and living conditions in Kolkata and move back to their villages after retirement (de Haan 2007). The persistence of smallholding agriculture in the region has also strengthened migrant workers' ties with land in their villages. For migrant men, their goal in coming to the city is to earn enough to send back money not just for everyday upkeep of their families but also to buy land and cattle (Mukherjee 2009).

This chapter dwells on taxi drivers' accounts of urban living to examine how modes of migrant masculine subjectivity are entwined with routines of city life. It aims to demonstrate how the experience of rural-to-urban migration and the itinerant character of cab driving frame working-class men's everyday geographies of risk in the city. Taxis in Kolkata—unlike autorickshaws—traverse the entirety of the city's landscape. This difference in scale of operation conditions migrant taxi drivers' inhabitations of urban risk. In attending to these concerns, the chapter conceptualizes masculine subjectivity as a terrain on which urban transformations are reflected. Since the 1990s, Bhojpuri cinema from Bihar has registered a telling transformation in its filmic ethos. In this time, the diegetic world of Bhojpuri cinema has placed considerable weight on the social environments of lower-caste, migrant laborers (Tripathy 2013). This new emphasis is reflected in the theme of urban-rural conflict that steers much of the narrative of Bhojpuri cinema in this period. The recurrent journey between village and city, the perceived threat of city cultures to rural identity, and the vagaries of urban living emerge as key tropes in film after film (Tripathy 2007). On the one hand, the recurrence of this theme in the cinema of the region underlines the significance of the migration experience for questions of identity in Bihar. On the other, dominant media representations of the Bihari migrant in urban middle-class Bengal construe Bhojpuri culture as vulgar and crass. The following comment from the transport minister, Madan Mitra, reported in an English daily in Kolkata, captures the cultural logic that is often levied to explain the Bihari migrant taxi drivers' incivility: "Most of the taxi drivers are not aware of Bengal's language and culture and the sentiment of local people and thus fail to provide them with the service they require." Such cultural evaluations of the male migrant signal Bihari taxi operators' contentious relationship to the city. Through an ethnographic assessment of their experiences of dislocation, community, sexuality, danger, and safety, this chapter situates migrant taxi drivers' mobile geographies in relation to mores of masculinity and the risks of urban living.

Being Migrant

Since the mid-1990s, the growing attention to masculinity in efforts to understand the gender social order has led cultural expectations from men to be incorporated in migration research. A number of studies have shown the various ways in which men's lives are inscribed by gender regimes and the migration process, examining the links between marriage and migration, rules of patrilocality and territorial exogamy, and how these influence migrant men's location in family relations (Thompson 2003; Agrawal 2006; Hibbins and Pease 2009; Charsley and Wray 2015). In the previous two decades, a vast body of scholarship has also theorized the role of cities in influencing migration flows (Holston and Appadurai 1999; Schiller and Çağlar 2009; Nicholls and Uitermark 2016). Much of this literature explicates the lure of prosperous cities for migrants for the economic opportunities they present and the complex social and political implications of this mobility. In India, studies of intercultural and interstate migration have had to contend with conflict between migrants' right to free movement within the country and territorial claims of ethnic nationalist groups (Blom Hansen 2001b). This chapter builds on understandings of gendered migration in urban spaces by reading public transport as a conduit of urban processes, everyday risk, and migrant male subjectivities.

If several migrant taxi drivers, such as Ram Prasad, recall their early days in the city as a brief phase of adventurous discovery and freedom from the strictures of work, the memories of a number of others dispute such a narrative. For Yogendra, who is now in his early forties and came to Kolkata when he was sixteen, his initial days in the city were spent washing cars, pleading with drivers to teach him how to drive, and desperately trying to find his feet in an unfamiliar milieu where support was seldom forthcoming. There were days when he went without meals, and Yogendra tears up as he recalls these early months. Like him, the urban memories of some migrant taxi drivers are those of hard labor, devoid of any form of care. Several drivers stressed that from these early experiences they quickly learned the value of saving money; life in the city taught them that. Hence, many claimed to not squander any money on alcohol, entertainment, or prostitution—wasteful expenses. It is difficult to earn good money, so they don't spend their wages on things they can go without.

In Kolkata slums, where many migrant taxi drivers live, speakers of Bengali and other Indian languages are often residentially segregated without much social interaction between linguistic groups (Shaw 2012). As such, the awareness of urban dislocation never leaves most migrant taxi operators. The passage of vast lengths of time in Kolkata, however, usually attenuates the intensity of such emotions. Initial months in the city are permeated by feelings of displacement, a sense of being removed from existing social networks. The sudden disappearance of strong emotional bonds from their lives provokes the need to return to their hometowns frequently. Daily food in the new location is both palatable and cheap but feels foreign on the tongue, as migrants crave meals in which every ingredient element is homemade. As the years pile on, however, the newness wears thin and the compulsion to frequent Bihar gradually abates. For some, the city that was once painfully new begins to resemble home, if only a temporary one. As a fifty-eight-year-old driver from Gaya district says, "These days, the city feels foreign only when one is traveling in a train between Bihar and Kolkata. Otherwise, it feels like home. I have some people I have got to know in these many years. I can call this city home these days. Earlier it was not possible."

On being asked to identify the major differences between their lives in the city and the villages in which they grew up, a few themes recurred in taxi drivers' narratives. Many spoke about the comfort of home-cooked food prepared by women in their families and noted that shifting to the city demands preparing one's own meals. Before their move to Kolkata, they were living with their families; this is what they return to every five or six months. In the city, they share a room with anything between five and ten other men; these men are often from the same village and are employed as taxi operators, construction workers, *paan* stall owners, or warehouse caretakers. While most eat out on a regular basis, there is often an agreement that every roommate, on his day off, cooks for the rest. The men I spoke to stressed that in Kolkata it is still affordable to purchase good-quality food from roadside hotels; in other cities this is too expensive. Many underlined this—easy access to affordable food, without having to undertake the hassle of cooking every day—as one reason for their preferring Kolkata over cities like Delhi and Mumbai, even though these locations promise higher earnings. Scholars (Shahidian 1999; Donaldson et al. 2009) have argued that migration compels men and women to rethink their prescribed gender roles and may even destabilize migrants' ideas about gender roles and the sexual division of labor. In the descriptions above we see how migrant men negotiate their attachments to male roles that are brought into crisis by the migration experience. The move away from one's family helps men to meet expectations of breadwinning even as it requires of them everyday tasks such as cooking and washing clothes that are feminized. While men may avoid some of these daily chores, in the context of their lives in the city this avoidance is more a reflex of male social habit than any obvious anxiety about feminization of certain forms of labor. As my conversations with migrant taxi operators revealed, the house rule of taking turns at cooking is arrived at without disagreements; and washing clothes can seldom be displaced onto others. In the single-gender household, away from their villages, there is a tacit understanding between men to share work traditionally performed by women. When asked if they would do housework in their villages, drivers promptly said they would not because these are not men's jobs and women in their families would take care of such matters. In an all-male household, the benefits of cooperation with other men exceed any unease about performing "women's work," whereas in a family household there is far greater male investment in upholding sexual divisions of labor. Physical dislocation from the family unit obliges negotiating with masculinity in ways that demonstrate another kind of "patriarchal bargain" (Kandiyoti 1988), wherein men perform certain feminized roles in their urban locations only to approximate patriarchal definitions of masculinity in the village. This suggests one kind of male reaction to gendered relations impelled by migration: involuntary introduction to domestic labor in the city appears to add mettle to migrant men's resolve to strengthen their dominance in the family sphere back in the village.

Much of the research on masculinity in contexts of migration highlights the hindrances that it generates for men to fulfil their social roles as men. Thus, men may find it difficult to find and keep jobs in the host society, thereby failing in their provider roles. They may also be compelled to commit to jobs that are underpaid or below their qualifications (Pease 2009). In their inability to meet dominant definitions of maleness, men may—through migration—lose some of their social power over women. For taxi drivers in Kolkata who have migrated from rural Bihar, their masculinities have a contradictory relationship with their mobility. While migration denudes them of some of the assurances they are used to as men, it also allows them to accomplish other conventional demands from masculinity. A thirty-eight-year-old taxi driver, originally from Saran district, recounts, "These days when I go back to Bihar I feel astonished sometimes. There is just no work. Either you work in the fields for money that is barely enough, or you just sit around. That is what the men who did not go anywhere do. That makes me glad about being in Kolkata; at least I get to earn here."

Mobility, therefore, is valuable not for itself but for allowing men to fulfill their provider role. The move to the city not only facilitates a tenuous approximation of a key index of masculinity but also creates an axis of differentiation between men who leave and those who stay behind. Inasmuch as mobility yields gainful employment, men both see themselves as respectable and accrue social prestige in the village upon relocating to the city. Such an evaluation cannot, however, be offered as a generality. One man's freedom is another's prison, and the journey to the city remains an ambiguous one. Consider this passionately expressed explanation of what it means to be a migrant: "Yes this city is foreign for us. We have left our wife and children, our parents, we are living alone far away. That is what you call being a migrant. Where are they and where am I? You live with your family. Do I not feel like doing the same? Do I not feeling like returning to my family after a hard day's work? I cannot. And that is what you call living in a foreign land. That's how I understand being a foreigner" (thirty-five-year-old migrant driver).

The desire for spatial rootedness and physical proximity to affinal kin shapes understandings of foreignness, revealing the degree to which men also make sense of their lives in the city through familial tropes. Thus, if some men create a narrative of respectability by tying male breadwinning to the city, others read their relocation as an imposition. It was impossible to miss the relish with which migrant taxi drivers spoke of sending regular remittances back home. But this sense of accomplishment would often also carry a sense of impending failure, as expenses rise every day and incomes do not. Indeed, migrant taxi drivers repeatedly stress the high costs of urban living, which disallow them from relocating their wives and children to the city. Studies have shown that, by migrating, men find themselves at odds with several social, educational, and institutional barriers that impede meeting the expectations of masculinity (Donaldson and Howson 2009). Such insecurities entailed in the migration experience may destabilize men's privilege in relation to the women in their families (Pessar 1999). The story of rural-urban migration that emerged in my interactions with taxi drivers in Kolkata conveyed a sense of how men avoid the potential loss of male social power that migratory experiences may impel. Migrant taxi drivers are unable to support their families in the city because of insufficient earnings, certainly; but another reason for this is that they consider it improper for women to participate in the labor force. They frequently invoke cultural scripts of rural life in Bihar—for instance, *dharm-naash*, or the sin of taking a woman of the house to the city—to authorize these gendered ideas of propriety. Their narratives create a prestige hierarchy in which they see their wives as being better positioned than working-class women laborers who have to toil in the city. Thus, in keeping their wives away from employment, this group of migrant men enable themselves to retain power over the women they have affinal relations with. It also allows them to position themselves as winners in an honor contest with local working-class men in the city, whom they often stigmatize for being unable to keep their wives at home.

It is worth emphasizing again the pattern of migration that taxi drivers from Bihar are embedded in. Taxi operators seldom spend more than four to six months at a stretch in Kolkata. Some return to their villages in Bihar only for a week or two, while others stay for as long as a couple of months. Such longer periods are spent helping out with farming. For generations, their families have done farm work, and so they learned it too as children. The regularity of these visits and the precarity of their professions mean that they see their lives in the city as temporary; they all know that once their health begins to fail and age catches up, they will have to return to their village. This particular circuit of mobility—which has been described as "sojourning" (Willis and Yeoh 2000)—means that migrant taxi drivers in Kolkata are simultaneously inserted within two gender regimes that structure their lives in the city and in the village. Migrant men carry ideas about gender relations from their hometowns into their new locations, even as this mobility forces them to confront some of their assumptions about masculinity (Howson 2009). It is revealing to consider some of the factors that provoke feelings of displacement in men and their part in constituting the urban experience. "We are migrants [*pardesi*], we have left our place to live in another place. That means we can be abused by a group of unruly men and we won't be able to do much. I have had many such experiences here" (forty-two-year-old operator from Vaishali district in Bihar).

Taxi drivers understand their vulnerability to abuse as a function of their immigrant status in Kolkata; they read it also as an effect of the mobile nature of their profession that impedes forming reliable social connections at work. Such narratives underline the ways in which migrant male subjectivity is produced as subordinate in relation to local versions of masculinity in the host city. As a community of strangers, the city is inhabited by rural migrant working-class men as a space of threat, of imminent violence from other (local) men. As this narrative and the opening vignette of this chapter suggest—"We were beaten up because we are from outside. They would not dare beat up a Bengali driver so easily. We are easy targets because we are alone here"—their immigrant status and the itinerant nature of their profession intersect to produce this sense of the city as a site where safety can be compromised at any moment. Many drivers actively manufacture a sense of security by reminding themselves that the economy of Bengal depends on the labor of men from Bihar, without whom the economy would simply collapse: "They can't get rid of us so easily." Taxi operators may invoke a collective "we" when speaking of their migration experience, but the absence of repeatable rituals makes their hold on a community identity especially tenuous. The presence of other men from their home villages might have prompted their journey to this city, but migrant taxi drivers' careers in the city allow only happenstance encounters, without the reiteration that is required to build affordances of community. Indeed, what distinguishes the city dwelling of the migrant taxi driver from other transport workers is his essential solitariness.

Over time, however, drivers develop a sense of the people whom they are most likely to face ill-treatment from. A thirty-six-year-old migrant taxi operator said, "This is a big city. There are all kinds of people here. Those who are educated, who have roamed and lived in different parts of the world, they do not consider us outsiders. But those who have never been outside, who has never felt the winds of distant lands, they are hostile to us. They have this tendency to abuse us for being here." Animosity toward Biharis is part of the broader social trend in which multiculturalism is seen by dominant groups in cities as a threat to known securities. It is noteworthy that rural men's move to the city and urban men's apprehensions that migrants will take away "their" jobs are partially based on anxieties about the loss of an important base of male power—employment. Thus, the conflict between migrant and local men is, at one level, a story of competing masculinities in the labor market. The linkages between place, mobility, work, and masculinity were brought out compellingly in this observation by a forty-seven-year-old migrant taxi driver: "We are men, so every place is fine for us. It has to be. Wherever men are they have to earn. So place is not important. But there is something about one's hometown. I would like to stay in Bihar, but there is no income there. Once my son is old enough to work, I will return."

The question of agency—to what extent movement is a choice—has been central to discussions about the politics of mobility (Dant 2014). Some working-class migrant men may identify non-attachment to place as a masculine characteristic by claiming that for them the pressures of breadwinning supersede place attachment; however, the tension between *is fine* and *it has to be* shows how such indices of maleness are actively produced as masculine rather than being a spontaneous reflex of male embodiment. The willingness to be mobile is yoked to masculinity through the ideology of male breadwinning, even as both—mobility and the compulsion to earn—sit uneasily on individual men. Thus, the vagaries of employment compel a reconsideration of what it means to be a man and men's relationship to mobility and space. Elspeth Probyn's (2003, 294) evocative words, "space presses against our bodies, and of necessity touches at our subjectivities," capture this idea that considerations of "who you are" cannot be addressed shorn of their relation to "where you are." As the narrative above shows, there is cultural sanction for men to express commitment to place only when they are past the age of employment, and this is achieved by displacing patriarchal demands from masculinity onto sons.

Relations with Auto Drivers

Auto drivers move within a zone. That is their strength. Where we taxis will go, we don't know. If someone decides to beat us up, they can do so easily. Be it passenger, or *mastan*, or police; we have no protection from anyone when we are out on the road.
—Forty-four-year-old migrant driver

Aspects of taxi drivers' inhabitations of the city are to be understood in terms of how the taxi relates to other modes of public transport in Kolkata. Transport workers' narratives invite attention to the different, yet overlapping, territorial reaches of the taxi and the autorickshaw and their implication for how masculinities are spatialized in the city. As we have seen in the previous chapter, autorickshaws in Kolkata follow fixed routes; taxis traverse the city and beyond. This difference in the pattern of mobility configures men's relationships to urban space and creates specific interactional dynamics between these two groups of transport workers. A forty-two-year-old taxi driver says,

> Auto drivers don't drive properly. Many of them drive without proper license. They regularly act smart with taxi drivers. They often declare grandly, "We operate within localities, you people have to roam the whole city." You can't park anywhere near their stand. Their union is tight. The taxi union isn't good. Everyone in it is a sellout. Today if the taxi union was strong they would not have allowed any other transport besides taxi and bus. The ministers also understand that our taxi union is no good. Auto drivers think they are tigers of their locality. When they go out of the locality they are not so confident anymore.

The social power that auto drivers are said to wield in relation to other transport workers derives entirely from their emplacement within specific localities. This geographic restriction becomes an enviable resource of transport work in the city in a number of ways. Since the routes on which auto drivers operate pass through localities they live in, they can rely on neighborly ties when under duress. For instance, apart from the tea stalls, which tend to cluster near autorickshaw bays, drivers may make a habit of stopping at others along their travel route and cultivate friendly relations with tea and *beedi* vendors. Similar friendly equations develop with other urban actors who work on the backstage of the transport infrastructural landscape in the city: car mechanics and filling station staff. In times of need, this fleeting sociality may harden into a structure of support for auto operators, a social relationship that the isolated nature of cab driving disallows. Some taxi drivers also become known and trusted to a few passengers. They may be entrusted, for example, to regularly ferry children of middle-class families to school and back home. Such trust relationships develop when taxi drivers are able to insert themselves into the sociability of neighborhood life. A taxi driver who is seen frequently in a particular neighborhood, waiting for passengers, becomes a familiar face; this familiarity allows neighborhood residents looking for mobility services to begin a conversation with the driver. If the negotiations prove fruitful, the driver and resident enter into a business relationship. These trust relationships involving taxi drivers, however, are much less frequent than those with autorickshaw drivers, whose trade is fundamentally structured by neighborhood relations. An auto driver recounted to me, for example, an incident involving the sudden breakdown of his vehicle as he was about to pick up his young son from school. Unable to abandon the vehicle, the driver importuned a teenage boy known to him from a tea stall he frequents to run the errand for him while he sought out a mechanic in the vicinity. On another occasion, I witnessed an auto driver pushing along another vehicle (that had broken down) with an outstretched leg while driving his own vehicle. Such forms of support, in addition to the camaraderie afforded by the social life of autorickshaws, inspire a spatial confidence that is wholly lacking in the careers of taxi drivers in the city, particularly among the many who are migrants. The use of a predatory metaphor—in the interview excerpt above—to describe the attitudes of auto drivers signals the aggressive and violent character such spatial confidence can assume. As a thirty-eight-year-old migrant taxi driver remembered, "I was driving on Dum Dum Road. One auto overtook me in a rough way and crashed into me. The driver came up and started fighting with me. A Bengali guy. He immediately called other auto drivers and started beating me. I was angry and sad that I got beaten up, but what could I do?"

The lack of such sociality among taxi operators and their immigrant status in the city have far-reaching repercussions for their transport labor. The nature of cab driving—which is solitary and takes operators to far-flung areas of the city—allows only a precarious sense of community among taxi drivers. This absence of a ritual of togetherness conditions their attitude to unionization, which contrasts starkly with the attitude of auto operators. While auto drivers generally repose a great deal of faith in their union, taxi drivers are united in their conviction that only politicians and a select few union leaders benefit from taxi associations. Drivers acknowledge the beneficial changes that a powerful union can bring to their profession, citing autorickshaw unions as an example, while also emphasizing their lack of community ties, which could strengthen unionization. As migrants, without many prior connections in the city, they are devoid of resourceful social networks that can help leverage political goals. The long history of migration from rural Bihar to urban Bengal appears to not have strengthened political participation in the city, at least among this group of migrant workers in the city. Moreover, as city dwellers who exercise their voting rights elsewhere in the country, they are overlooked in the calculations of political patronage that influence urban informalities in India. The finitude of migrant operators' stay in the city—which involves regular trips back to Bihar, often for extended lengths of time—also weakens the resolve to unionize and invest in political action in Kolkata.

Crime and Safety

Fear is a locality-related issue.
—Thirty-seven-year-old driver

The fear of crime and therefore concerns about personal safety pervade the working lives of taxi drivers. Their experiences on city streets and fearsome stories reported by others serve as the principal pedagogical sources of urban danger and security. While such apprehensions of harm construe particular neighborhoods and peoples as disorderly and susceptible to violence, the fall of darkness is generally presented by taxi operators as the harbinger of iniquity in the city. These narratives of fear and safety provide occasion to think about the making of masculine subjectivities in the context of the fear-risk nexus. Feminist criminological research has amply demonstrated that the majority of crimes are committed by men and that, despite widespread violence against women, men are far more violent toward each other (Stanko 1994). Moreover, men's unwillingness to admit weakness results in considerable disparity between the extent of male victimization and their reports of experiencing fear (Newburn and Stanko 1994). Such empirical findings have necessitated wrestling with the links between cultural expectations of masculinity and crime (Tomsen 2008). Using these insights, this subsection of the chapter calls for more specific attention to issues of masculinity in relation to urban fear, in particular by considering its relationship to everyday mobility. The discussion that follows focuses on feelings of fear and safety to unravel social relations between men in the city and places particular emphasis on how movement through urban spaces configures these urban affects. It shows how the pervasiveness of men's violence toward other men makes it impossible to speak of men's relationship to the city as one of unhindered access alone.

Once in Park Circus at eleven o'clock at night, criminals got up in my car. I saw them taking out pistols and other sharp weapons from a box. I saw but pretended that I have not noticed. I knew there are police patrols in that area in the crossroad. I told them I have to pee. I approached the police and told them sir there are criminals in my car. They went and immediately arrested them. I needed to get to an area where I would find support. Either the public or the police. (thirty-one-year-old taxi driver)

Taxi drivers' highly irregular geographies of movement mean that they cannot depend on the presence of other operators and have to actively identify other structures of support in public spaces. The severity of the hazard often determines what sort of help is sought and from whom. Thus, if in the situations described above the driver approaches the police for support, in other instances it may well be law enforcement officers themselves whom taxi operators need to avoid to be safe. Hence, in the laboring lives of taxi drivers, there is considerable investment in sensing danger in public spaces. A twenty-nine-year-old driver explains, "This one time, in Alipore, criminals were looking out to hire a taxi. A few of them had bikes. They started following me. I understood they are criminals. We are taxi drivers, we know who is who. His body cutting, his face, his way of carrying himself, these things tell us what he is about. Your body language and criminals' body language are totally different."

Just as in the middle-class imaginary transport workers come to embody disobedience and lawlessness, workers themselves have their own understanding of unruliness in the city that they use to manufacture personal security. Being outdoors for as long as taxi drivers are requires directing efforts at creating a mental map for being safe in the city and assessing in which contexts the risk of victimization is high. The manufacture of safety entails a calculus of space.

> Yes, there are areas in the city where I feel afraid to go. Metiabruz [predominantly Muslim neighborhood] I generally avoid. I have not faced anything. But I have heard stories. This guy I know was attacked in that area, his money, his phone were forcibly taken away. Some people are in this sort of business. They will say, "Will you go to Metiabruz?" And then in the middle of the route, when you cross Khidirpur, some other guys will get up. Then they start snatching your money, phone, whatever you are carrying, hitting you. Who wants to deal with all this? (forty-year-old Hindu driver)

Migrant taxi drivers—including those who identify as Muslim—routinely associate poor Muslim neighborhoods in the city with danger and crime. The social makeup of these neighborhoods highlights the sociospatial exclusions through which Muslims experience urban life in Kolkata. Muslims are concentrated in "slum wards" in the eastern region of the city, in wards in central Kolkata "characterized by narrow lanes, crumbling housing, and little sign of buoyant real estate development" (Shaw 2012, 107), and in a few neighborhoods (such as Metiabruz) along the western riverfront. These localities often have high rates of male unemployment and low levels of literacy, suffer from delinquency and drug addiction, and are populated by residents who are mostly involved in short-term jobs in the informal sector (Shaw 2012). Migrant taxi drivers' stories of violent encounters in the city capture the frictional interplay between locality, mobility, and danger through which two versions of masculine otherness are produced—male victimhood to other men's criminal behavior and the threatening masculinity of poor Muslim youth.

In expressing their sense of fear in urban spaces, taxi operators narrate a changing crime profile of the city through the years. They recall a time—some thirty years ago—when they would instantly refuse passengers who wished to travel to the precincts of the city. Areas such as Salt Lake in the northeast and Kasba in the south were zealously avoided on account of their disrepute as crime-infested zones. The fear was as much of petty crime as of becoming a collateral victim of male-to-male homicide and gang violence. The identification of these localities with crime and violence changed with the construction of the Eastern Metropolitan Bypass and commercial developments along it on the eastern fringes of the city through the 1990s. A fifty-three-year-old driver remembers,

Kolkata was such a small city, now I see how large it has become. In front of my eyes I have seen, before twenty to thirty years people would not go to Salt Lake out of fear. There was a tiny lane connecting salt lake to the city. Behala, Thakurpukur; what were these areas! You feared robbers and *goondas*. Now everything is city. I remember seeing a guy running with a huge sword, no one was being able to control him. I saw him just slice someone on his way and escape into a narrow lane in Kasba [predominantly lower-middle-class Hindu neighborhood]. Even back then I was a taxi driver. We used to have helpers back then. You had to save your own life in such situations!

The dwindling career of the helper provides an index to the changing social standing of the taxi driver in Kolkata. In the face of such widespread crimes in the city, the helper was quite literally a figure of support for the taxi driver. The helper was typically someone who wanted to join the taxi industry as a driver and used this opportunity to learn the trade and familiarize himself with the roads. The understanding was that the taxi driver would provide him two meals a day and teach him to drive, while the presence of the helper would afford him some security. A couple of factors made the helper redundant to the taxi driver. First, as violent crimes were brought under control, the hazards for the driver were reduced significantly. Second, the helper gradually slipped away from the side of the driver as the duo came to be perceived as potential criminals themselves. Passengers, particularly women, would refuse to hire a taxi that had a helper. Since the presence of the helper began to harm business, he was dispensed with. The disappearance of the helper shows the transformation in the cultural meanings ascribed to the figure of the taxi driver. From someone in need of protection, the driver becomes someone whom the middle classes require protection from. Thus, from being in danger, he becomes dangerous himself. This shift in reputation needs to be understood also in terms of the changing social profile of taxi drivers, specifically the perceived differences between the Sikh and Bihari communities. An editorial published in the *Telegraph* in 2004 sees its upper-class Anglo-Indian writer ruing the diminution of the city's number of Sikh taxi drivers, who are perceived to be sincere and well-meaning. He recalls, fondly, an oft-repeated moment in his childhood: his mother telling him, when he implored her for a taxi fare instead of the usual tram ride, "*Beta*, as long as you find a Sardarji's taxi . . . you will be safe in his hands." The disrepute that has gathered around the figure of the taxi driver is, therefore, also to be explained by the ascription of notoriety to men from rural Bihar, in stark contrast with the honest reliability of Sikh masculinity.

Any discussion of taxi drivers' experiences of crime in the city must necessarily give due consideration to urban nights. The

growing scholarship on the nighttime city has routinely remarked on the speedy recession of the limits imposed by darkness on human activity (Melbin 1978). Indeed, the sheer range of facilities that are now open at night—entertainment venues and transport, news, hospitality, and medical services—makes it sensible to speak of a distinct economy of the city after dark. Much of this literature, itself focused on a few North American, British, and

Australian cities, has underlined the centrality of nighttime leisure to revitalizing postindustrial urban economies (Roberts and Eldridge 2012). Taxi drivers' accounts of the nocturnal city signal, tangentially, some of this same shift in cities of the Global South but largely demonstrate the continuing association of the nighttime city not so much with consumption-oriented leisure practices but with vice and danger: "At night, *chengra* people [loafers] give trouble. They are out to steal at night. My fear is of bad people, that anyone can come beat us up. So I don't like driving after nine thirty" (thirty-one-year-old driver).

Inasmuch as all public spaces are cast as dangerous for women, the city after dark is deemed especially unsafe. Tack Back the Night initiatives led by women's activists are therefore part of a larger struggle to wrest from men the exclusive right to the city, including the city at night. Feminist writer Andrea Dworkin notes, in a 1970 pamphlet from one such Take Back the Night venture, that the "night is magical for men. They look for prostitutes and pickups at night. They do their so-called lovemaking at night. They get drunk and roam the streets in packs at night. They f-ck their wives at night. They have their fraternity parties at night. They commit their so-called seductions at night." Such ascriptions of abandon to men's lives in the nocturnal city are not borne out by the lives of taxi drivers. In fact, taxi drivers' descriptions of the nighttime city unfailingly associated darkness with their vulnerability to harm. As a forty-seven-year-old driver explains, "At night no good person goes out in the street. The *bhadra* [decent] person is not out after ten o'clock. You never know what kind of person you encounter at night. It's Kolkata city, there are so many kinds of people here. Alcoholics, robbers they are most out after dark. Who knows what happens when?"

While the city is inherently unpredictable, this uncertainty presents particular kinds of threats once night falls. It would be a mistake to treat this association between darkness and depravity as conservative moralism alone; rather, these experiences of insecurity also tell a more significant story about gendered attitudes to the times and spaces of the city. Taxi operators claim, for instance, that driving a public vehicle at night makes specific demands of personality; one has to be a certain type of person to adequately grapple with the city after dark. "I am not the right person to drive at night. I can't abuse and fight so much. Someone who has the energy for all that, he can drive at night. At night the big problem is alcohol. Once people have drunk too much you don't know what they will say or do to you. I don't have the temperament to haggle with difficult people" (thirty-nine-year-old driver).

Thus, while the literature on the nighttime urban economy emphasizes leisure and entertainment, for transport workers in urban India the nocturnal city remains something that needs to be survived. It requires specific modes of self-conduct and dispositions toward others, a willingness to manage the particular challenges thrown up by the nighttime city. With the passage of day into night, the forms of social control that rein in disruptive elements during the day are perceived to recede and the unruly erupts onto urban space. This particular case reveals how by pathologizing alcohol consumption and drunkenness as a criminal problem, two ideas of masculinity are produced—a soft masculinity that is vulnerable to drunken violence and an aggressive masculinity that has the mettle to withstand such abuse in the city after dark. Of course, drunkenness is only one factor in creating feelings of vulnerability in the city at night. Another is the lone woman who has dared to venture outdoors in the dark.

This was when I would drive at night, some ten to fifteen years ago. It was two o'clock. I saw a woman. Late twenties, married, wearing a saree. She asked me to take her to Garia station. I got scared. [Why did you get scared?] At two o'clock, a lone woman, she can harm me I thought. One has to think of good and bad when on the road. Maybe she takes me to her locality and gets me beaten up. Maybe accuses me of molesting her. Who knows? There are deceptive women; they may steal from you and then accuse you of molestation. I asked her, "Why are you out so late? Are you in trouble?" She said she was fine. I thought she is running away from her husband after a fight or something. I didn't speak much. After I dropped her she said she had no money. I told her, "Whoever's house you are going to ask them to pay? Surely you won't be out the whole night? Tell your brother, mother, whoever you are visiting to pay me." She refused to budge from there, so I came away. What could I do at that hour, no one was around! She asked me where I stay. The next day, in the morning, she came and paid the fare. I was sleeping inside the car; she woke me up. One can try to assess people, but whether that will be correct is impossible to say beforehand.

Women who are outdoors at night both are precarious and provoke precarity in men. "Why are you out so late? Are you in trouble?" suggests that the lone woman in the nighttime city is seen by most men as either vulnerable or as a threat. A woman's sartorial markers—in this case of marriage—may appeal to an ethic of male protectionism, but she continues to be seen as an enticement. To adapt Elizabeth Wilson's (1991) oft-quoted words, one may say that even when a woman is not read as a whore, she remains a temptress, with the power to lure men into peril. Indeed, stories of women ensnaring unsuspecting men in the late hours of the city abound in taxi drivers' accounts of urban nights. Such scenes and stories provide for men a deeply gendered pedagogy of danger and safety on city streets. When women's presence in public spaces at night is framed as an anomaly, it simultaneously construes them as powerful and men as likely victims of this power. And yet the inherent indeterminacy in knowing the city, of telling bad from good, safety from danger, means that men seldom derive the same lessons from the everyday tutelage of streets. Will she cause harm? Or is she herself in danger? These learnings depend as much on social locations of urban actors as on their individual dispositions. It is necessary to highlight that both sets of reactions—protectiveness and fear—stem from a masculinist understanding of public spaces as ill-suited for women. As the anecdote above suggests, the denouements of some city encounters may weaken the second of these impressions and make it seem sensible to repose a bit of faith in the goodness of strangers.

It has been argued that for many men, particularly those who feel undermined, violence becomes the principal mode of expressing and validating masculine identity (DeKeseredy and Schwartz 2005). The narratives on crime and safety documented in this subsection show the part played by cultures of violent masculinity in producing the outdoors, particularly after night, as unsafe for men. It is interesting to note, moreover, that inasmuch as violence becomes a mode of proving masculinity, the ability to manage other men's violence also emerges as a criterion for a socially valued form of maleness. In the context of rural-to-urban migration that underpins this chapter, this valuation of masculinity exhibits particular dynamics of ethnic contestation between men. As a thirty-four-year-old taxi operator from rural Bihar claimed, "Bengalis are not ready to be drivers. There are great risks to driving a taxi. There will be accidents, the vehicle will break down, the public will beat you up, the police will harass you. Bengalis are scared. Bihari men are habituated to taking risks in life. We know how to handle problem situations."

In an urban milieu that routinely stigmatizes him, the disenfranchised male migrant deploys other systems of cultural evaluation—in this case, colonial ascriptions of effeminacy to the Bengali man (Sinha 1995)—to legitimize his presence in the city: the supposedly civilized Bengali man is also effete and hence ill-suited to handle the tempestuous flows of urban uncertainty.

Sexual Lives

A single man in his mid-twenties and a married woman in her thirties are in the midst of a lovers' tiff. She is upset and the man draws her toward him to comfort her. The situation has become unbearable for her. Her husband is suddenly overwhelmed with suspicion. Each time she is away from the city, he is convinced that she is with her lover. He has proof, he says, of all the clandestine trips she has made. His suspicions have made him sexually aggressive toward her; she shows him the marks on her neck. The young man is distraught to learn that she still sleeps with her husband and pushes her away. She tries to make him understand that as a married woman she can't refuse sex to her husband endlessly.

This intimate moment—portrayed in the 2006 Bengali film *Dosar* (The companion)—transpires inside a moving taxi and hints at some of the meanings that the urban middle classes ascribe to the vehicle and its operator. The interior of the taxi is treated as a private enclave, which allows personal conversations not easily conducted elsewhere. But the same space can become oppressive, restricting freedom of movement if the exchange becomes cruel; in the scene described above, both lovers attempt to alight mid-journey when the conversation becomes hurtful. Of particular interest to our discussion here is how behavior inside a cab configures the presence of the male taxi driver. For the interior of the vehicle to emerge as a zone of personal interaction, the architecture of the car is useful but not sufficient; the presence of the driver has to be discursively annulled. The middle-class clientele of the taxi achieves this by invalidating the social judgments of the working classes. The kind of conversation we witness in the film is possible only in a taxi—and not an autorickshaw or a mass transit system—because its only other occupant is someone whose opinion doesn't matter. What remains of the driver is his working-class male sexuality, construed as lascivious. In the scene described above, the taxi driver is shown repeatedly turning back with sexual interest when the woman pulls backs her hair to show her lover the marks on her neck. Thus, if in the private spaces of the middle-class Bengali home the sexuality of male domestic workers can be temporarily effaced (Ray 2000), in the outdoors the working-class migrant man's lust is ever-present. This sexual characterization of the figure of the taxi driver is also related to the decline of Sikh involvement in the taxi industry in Kolkata and the concomitant growth of transport workers from rural Bihar.

One strand in public discussions of violence against women in public spaces has framed the problem in terms of a clash of values between upwardly mobile middle-class women and working-class, rural migrant men unable to handle this new version of urban Indian femininity. As Amrute (2015, 332) writes, "A new social and economic relationship is at work in cars that depends on lower-class men as dangerous subjects even while it makes their labor invisible." Mainstream media reportage is rife with stories of taxi drivers masturbating while ferrying women passengers, threatening/committing rape, and physically assaulting hapless middle-class commuters. The issue, of course, is not that such forms of harassment and assault do not take place; indeed they do, as the experiences of women in cities adequately document. Rather, the problem lies in dominant representations of public assault that characterize it as a specifically working-class male impulse. Consequently, one seldom encounters newspaper reports of such routine harassment within members of the middle class. In building the moral reputation of social groups in these totalizing ways, these representations also miss the different modes of self-conduct that men practice in the course of urban living to manage the problem of sexuality. This oversight is observable also in feminist writings on cities that, in demonstrating the basic structural inequality between genders, cast cisgender heterosexual men solely as potential aggressors in public space. A feminist reading of urban life that is informed by an awareness of the "psychic life of power" (Butler 1997) would also be interested in the points at which structures of domination fail to fully constitute sexual subjectivities. Here, an ethnographic account can be useful in capturing migrant men's textured responses to urban sexuality and convey an erotic topography of the city that isn't subsumed by a language of hostility.

"Yes we see so much sexual intimacy between men and women here. It is the culture of cities, of the times. It makes no difference to me. I mean, there is no point being tempted by something that I just will not get. Why crave for it? I will never get it, so why run my mind after it?" (twenty-eight-year-old taxi driver). Working-class migrant men often cultivate an attitude of indifference to erotic interactions they encounter in cities, particularly those that their class location forbids them from experiencing firsthand. This ethic of indifference develops also because, in the matter of sex/romance, most migrant drivers do not locate their sexual subjectivity in the time-space of the city—"It is the culture of cities, of the times. It makes no difference to me." Indeed, the culture of rural Bihar, in which taxi operators spent their early years, continues to exercise enormous influence on their sexual and romantic careers in Kolkata. In speaking about their sexual longings, a number of taxi operators stressed that it is customary in rural Bihar for people to marry at a young age. Thus, if most arrive in the city to find work on the cusp of adulthood, they get married within a year or two of beginning to earn. The general value attached to monogamy means that taxi operators are not single for long enough to experiment with their sexuality in the city. Moreover, as a forty-two-year-old married taxi operator from Gaya district recounted, "In our place, if there is love marriage the lovers are killed. I got some chances here with women, but I did not pursue them. Because women here don't know how to do farm work. In my place you need hands that know how to work in the fields. Women here will not like to do such work. They are used to buying cooking ingredients from the shop, but in Bihar women make everything from scratch with their hands."

Several migrant drivers also emphasized the economy of romance, reasoning that erotic involvement with city women requires disposable income, something that poor men do not have access to. They therefore quickly learned to curtail any sexual longing they might have felt in the interest of providing sufficiently for their families in rural Bihar. These narratives suggest that the erotic provocations of city life lead migrant men to relearn how to manage sexual desire, learnings that are structured by ideas of male and family honor. Mukul, a twenty-one-year-old taxi operator from Gaya district, told me, "Even if news of a small matter about something that I have done here goes back home, my parents will commit suicide out of shame. So I stay clear of wrong paths." A great deal of writing on the so-called freedom of city life is premised on the idea of anonymity and escape from community rules of the village. The long history of working-class labor migration from rural Bihar to Kolkata renders the cloak of anonymity ineffective. As the regular traffic of workers threatens to carry stories from the city to the village, the gender regime of rural life remains compelling in the city.

For the majority of taxi operators I spoke to, their sexualities remained contained within the boundaries of marriage. For this reason, the management of sexuality in the city has much to do with them living away from their wives. Many drivers prefer operating a taxi over a private car precisely because the latter has stricter rules about vacation time; in the taxi industry, being away for a week or so every two to three months is easily negotiable. The relative nearness of Kolkata to their hometowns makes the city a preferable working destination for these men from rural Bihar. In reflecting on their sexual lives in the city, many migrant drivers remembered, particularly in the early years of their marriage, returning for extended periods of time to their villages whenever the desire to have sex arose. The details of everyday sexual conduct of poor migrant men in the city sharply contradict their representation in the middle-class imaginary as rapacious and the principal threat to middle-class women's safety in the city. A thirty-eight-year-old driver says, "It isn't much of a struggle living separately from my wife. I am sure even for my wife it is not a problem. We are not like that; we know how to endure [bardasht]. What can you do if you are in a foreign land? Our wives also have the capacity to endure; they understand. Immediately after my wedding, I stayed with my wife back at home continuously for two years. I would return more often, till our children were born."

Physical distance obliges working-class migrant men to cultivate a habit of withholding desire, which makes the deprivation of life in the city—away from their wives—more bearable. Such habitual living with unfulfilled sexual longing is made easy on account of the kind of valued personhood that it implies. The management of sexuality in these terms serves to forge a masculine self-understanding that is able to present itself as respectable in an urban climate that routinely stigmatizes him. We must note, however, that taxi operators display a wide variety of attitudes to urban sexuality that cannot, therefore, be rendered monolithically in terms of an ethic of sexual abnegation. I asked Ranjan, forty-three, from Begusarai, if he has had sexual/romantic relations in Kolkata:

> Earlier prostitutes used to stand on the main roads. If I liked anyone I would pick them up. I would pay and have sex. [Wasn't space an issue?] Yes, now there are problems, earlier there was no problem. The city used to be empty, less people. You could go to a deserted area and do your thing. I remember we would park our vehicle on Park Street and just go to sleep on lazy days. Earlier there weren't so many policemen also. I stopped doing all this when my children were born. The father's sins fall on his children.

Thus, shifts in the nature of urban policing and men's changing roles within the family coalesce to influence erotic opportunities in the city. Research on young fatherhood often narrates the experience of becoming a father as a story of transition from youthful recklessness to adult responsibility (Reeves 2006). The interview excerpt above attaches one meaning of responsible fatherhood to sexual conduct and shows the continuing influence of the Vedic idea that the sins of parents are visited upon their children. Keshav, an upper-caste, fifty-six-year-old driver from Madhubani district, shares,

> Some women did approach me. They would say, "Should I come along with you for a bit? See the city with you." I would say, "No, people from my village will see I am roaming with girls, they will shame me back home." These women are mostly domestic servants [*jhi*]. I did desire some of them, but I did not want to get involved. She cleans other people's utensils, must be having other people's *jhootha* [what is soiled or already tasted by another person, and hence considered defiled], how do you kiss a woman like that every day, as your wife? If I take a woman like

that back home people will shame me, saying, "See he married a domestic servant, someone who handles other people's soiled utensils." They will evaluate her poorly, I will not like it.

Migrant men's dual emplacement in the social worlds of city and village make available certain erotic opportunities and require that these be assessed with due consideration to the codes of rural life. The solitude of the migrant taxi driver and his easy mobility make him sexually appealing to a certain female labor group in the city. But here we encounter the interruption of sexual pursuit not by an ethic of self-control but by caste-based notions of purity and pollution. Keshav continues, "As taxi drivers we see what city people do. Be they old or young, men and women get up on the car and stick to each other. The man wraps his arms around her and keeps pressing to see if they are ripe or not. Yesterday it was tight, why is it loose today? I can't lie to you, I find it entertaining to watch all this!"

This bawdy account discloses an often-overlooked aspect of the erotics of the city—the pleasure of looking. Understandings of lust in public spaces ought not to be constrained within the tactile and instead accommodate the visual as a mode of urban pleasure sufficient unto itself. Indeed, a couple of distinguishing elements of a specifically urban sexuality are its visuality and notional abundance (Bech 1998). This has to do with the large number of bodies of strangers in public spaces that are mostly available in the form of surfaces to be viewed (Bech 1998). The narrative excerpted above signals an erotic pleasure that rests entirely on optic involvement with strangers. One may also note—with reference to the taxi—a further aspect of this interplay between visuality and the abundance of erotic supply in cities: the ephemerality of viewing pleasure, which promises repetition in terms of the sexual script being played out on the rear view mirrors, but not the same actors. Indeed, attention must also be drawn to the architecture of the vehicle, particularly the function of mirrors in facilitating this erotic theater. The rearview mirrors make the driver's gaze on his passengers indirect, and it is this indirection that allows the interior of the taxi to be treated by passengers as a quasi-private place and a somewhat bashful spectatorship. The visual, I would argue, is especially meaningful in the erotic life of the subaltern urban male for whom the upper-class, "Westernized" woman is available mostly as an image. The field of erotic imagery—be it in vernacular pornographic material (Srivastava 2013) or in the lived world—emerges, particularly for the subaltern urban male, as the principal terrain on which an unattainable object of desire can be relished. Indeed, the discursive fashioning of sexual subjectivities signals the contestations between local and migrant masculinities in urban space. Consider this boastful declaration by a forty-five-year-old migrant taxi driver: "Immediately after marriage, I would spend two months in Kolkata, two months back home. When I would be home I would f-ck three times every night. City men can f-ck for only five minutes, then they orgasm. We f-ck continuously for half hour; we won't let ourselves orgasm. Men here are like leaky pens that keep dripping."

The extensive literature on rurality and gender has demonstrated how ideas of control over land and nature become a key trope of masculinity in the contexts of farming and rural life (Little 2002). In the account shared above, this theme of control is brought to the domain of sexual performance to fashion rural masculinity as more virile than that of city men. By constructing such mythologies of sexual prowess, rural and migrant identities are simultaneously invoked to privilege rural-migrant masculinity over urban forms of maleness. The use of such "compensatory masculine self-images" (Poynting, Tabar, and Noble 2009, 141) is common in the making of migrant male subjectivities that are often disadvantaged in the host society.

If some drivers find pleasure in watching sexual intimacy between passengers, others bring a certain prohibitive moralism to the idea of sex in a public vehicle: "I see couples trying to have quick sex in the taxi. Woman performs oral sex on the man. I ask them to get off when I see all this. This car is not for f-cking, it's for taking people to different places. I and my family eat thanks to this car. If you want to f-ck you can go to a hotel."

Here too we note an idiom of purity (the taxi) and pollution (sex) mediating conceptions of the proper use of public transport facilities. But in this instance the sacredness of the taxi rests foundationally on its part in sustaining drivers' families. The invocation of the sacred in talk about men's provider role underlines the sheer ideological force behind masculinity's attachment to breadwinning. Indeed, moral understandings of the function of the taxi inflect operators' responses to the general climate that connects the problem of rape in public spaces to working-class masculinity. A number of taxi operators suggested that drivers who commit rape ought to be killed. These assertions are based on a certain pattern of moral reasoning: "Taxi drivers are supposed to serve the public. Not only are you not helping the public, instead you are harming them? It's very wrong!" (forty-year-old taxi driver).

Thus, taxi drivers derive a moral basis for their labor also from seeing themselves as public service providers. In this narrative, sexual violence is discouraged not by any idea about women's right to their bodies but by a general ethic of public good that frames, normatively, the task of cab driving. One of the reasons for emphasizing a diversity of worldviews among men has been to identify avenues for transforming masculinity into egalitarian forms of gender (Connell 1995). The passage from multiplicity to change is, however, not an inevitable one as diverse forms of masculinity may conform in different ways to patriarchal definitions of maleness.

Conclusion

The specter of danger is a constant companion of the solitary taxi driver. In this sense, despite the long years spent navigating the city, taxi drivers remain unaccustomed to its streets. As migrants traversing the expansive geography of cab driving, taxi operators are repeatedly exposed to the inherent unknowability of the city. Surviving the streets, therefore, requires gathering knowledge about which spaces, people, and institutions will harm and which will offer protection. Keeping safe in the outdoors entails learning, through experiences and anecdotes, about the likelihood of danger and the competence to cope with it. Taxi operators realize that one can never understand the ways of the city enough, and hence the street's lessons remain fallible. The risk of harm is a perpetual presence in migrant working-class men's mobilities in the city, and such risk encompasses threats to body, dignity, and the moral self as well as institutional intimidations.

Taxi drivers' identification and management of urban danger provide a lens through which to grasp the making of masculinities at the crossroads of risk and movement in the city. At the intersection of taxi drivers' risk knowledges about who is dangerous, where, and when, and who is vulnerable, a set of gendered urban identities are created: the migrant male who is vulnerable to abuse from locals; the effete local man who is not able to handle dangerous scenarios; the migrant who can weather urban violence; the Muslim male with a propensity for lawlessness; the vulnerable woman on the street and the gallant man; the temptress and the entrapped male. These gendered urban identities exist on a capacity scale of who can inflict harm and who can protect both himself and deserving others. Such forms of masculinity and femininity in urban spaces are produced by everyday reflexes to mobility and risk. In other words, taxi drivers' movements through urban spaces and their management of risk give rise to recognizable gender identities in the city. These gendered identities convey the interpretive frameworks migrant working-class men use to make sense of what it means to live and work in the city.

The many unknowns of the city carry the possibility of danger for the taxi driver. But the unknowns may also bring joy; and there is pleasure too, in playing with and subduing danger. The careers of migrant taxi drivers suggest that the uncertainty of urban life positions men as risk takers and hence urges them to identify risk makers in the city. The inherent indeterminacy of the modern city makes men's experiences of risk assume a particular character: if men have to show a readiness to risk harm, a willingness to take on dangerous tasks in order to be valued (Seidler 2006), the city, in its expansive unknowability, emerges as the primary arena for men's risky behavior; it allows men the self-affirming pleasure of knowing that they can tackle threats to body and identity without being paralyzed by the prospect of urban danger.

Cab drivers at a taxi bay on a major thoroughfare sit on the ground playing cards. I watch them from a nearby bench for a while, noticing the difference in the nature of sociability between this gathering of taxi drivers and autorickshaw drivers in Kolkata. After a while, I join them for a round of cards, saying I am waiting for a friend who is running late. I sit among them for nearly an hour; the conversation is mostly about the game itself, interspersed with stray comments about an international one-day cricket match scheduled for the following day. I once again note the impersonality of these interactions, devoid of the banter—even ribaldry—that I routinely witnessed among autorickshaw drivers. On one occasion, while I was hanging out at an autorickshaw depot, I heard one driver tell another jokingly, "I hear you have fever for some days? You need to stop masturbating; you are overdoing it I think." On another hot summer day, I heard an autorickshaw driver walk toward a group of operators, asking for water. One man's reply—"Sure I have water, but why do I feel you won't like my water [implying semen]?"—sent them all into peals of laughter. This sort of lewd humor conveys the intimacy that autorickshaw drivers are able to forge among themselves as they do the work of transport labor. Compared to such sexualized humor among auto drivers, when I hired the taxi driven by one of the operators who were playing cards that day and asked him about his relationship with his peers, he said that he does not even know any of their names and has no idea when he will see them again, if ever. They were incidentally all waiting for passengers at that taxi stand that day and decided to play cards to pass the time.

These interactions hint at the kinds of homosocialities that evolve between different groups of public transport workers in the city. In the next chapter, I elaborate what homosociality has to do with traffic policing.

4
Homosocial Trust

Traffic Police

Scene 1

When I hailed this taxi on a sultry summer afternoon in Kolkata, the vehicle was already occupied; but its passengers were about to alight. The taxi had carried some large equipment, and from the conversation I gathered that the driver had asked for an extra INR30 for this service. The passengers did not have enough money on them to pay him and told the driver that they needed to go indoors to fetch the sum. They had alighted on a major street in the city, and the driver became visibly afraid about having to wait for long in that spot where he was likely to be nabbed by traffic police. As more time passed and we waited for his previous passengers to return with the fare, the driver grew more and more restless, caught between the impulse to leave that spot and the need to stay on to earn an extra buck.

Scene 2

As I was waiting inside an autorickshaw one afternoon for the vehicle to get its full complement of four passengers, a traffic sergeant walked up to the autorickshaw operator. The sergeant addressed the driver by his first name and began chastising him for waiting at a major crossroad, an offence for which he should be fined. The operator stepped out of the vehicle and began mock pleading with the police officer, telling him that he has promised his wife tickets to a film. If he is made to pay a hefty fine, he would be unable to keep his promise: "You are married yourself, sir, you know the damages of failing to keep a promise to your wife, please don't fine me." The sergeant guffawed and asked the operator to drive off immediately and ensure that he does not commit such traffic offences in the future.

The labor geographies of public transport vehicle operators in Kolkata are routinely marked by encounters with traffic police. In the course of their daily travels, transport workers cannot take for granted a right to labor in the city; instead, they have to seize that right through repeated confrontations with traffic law enforcement officers. The overlaps and differences between the social profiles of different groups of public transport workers, the geographical limits of their trades, and the discrete legal status of different modes of public transport in Kolkata complicate their encounters with urban traffic policing. As we have seen, while all transport workers are working-class men, autorickshaw drivers are primarily "locals" who follow only specific neighborhood routes, whereas most taxi drivers are migrants from nearby states in eastern India who roam the entire landscape of the city. Furthermore, while the taxi has a presence in the Motor Vehicles Act 1988 as a contract carriage, the autorickshaw has no mention in this act of the Parliament of India that governs road transport vehicles in the country. Instead, the operation of autorickshaws as a form of shared paratransit has been regularized by a set of state government rules and high court decisions. These social and legal bases of public transportation in Kolkata provide the ground for negotiations between forms of labor and state monitoring practices that are understood in urban theory as informality. For the urban middle class, traffic problems are explained habitually with reference to unruly driving practices of transport workers alone, and the relationship between them and the police is usually understood through two frames: either the public transport vehicle driver is a clever "rogue" who eludes the reach of law or the city police are seen as their accomplices and not responsible public servants. And yet often the situation develops that taxi drivers have been fined so excessively by traffic police that they go off the road in fear and there is a taxi shortage in the city.

The exercise of social control in cities has historically been linked to a wide variety of policing mechanisms in urban contexts. The critical tradition in urban studies has, for the most part, understood the relationship between urban policing and disenfranchised social groups in the city as an antithetical one. However, the everyday contexts in Kolkata in which the metropolitan police and men situated on the urban margins interact reveal a social relationship that braids cooperation with conflict. As the first of the two scenes outlined above showcases, public transport workers are regularly pushed into situations in which trying to earn a living inevitably entails coming up against the rule of law. Hence, there is a perpetual sense of frenzy while being out on the streets, generated by the conflict between the need to earn and the risk of getting apprehended by police. However, as the second vignette conveys, this conflictual relationship coexists with cooperative ties with law enforcement officers. Transport workers and traffic police also forge sociable relations with one another. What do these often-overlooked moments of cooperation and sociability between state actors and marginalized urban laborers tell us about gendered social inequality in the city?

Through descriptions of quotidian interactions of conflict and cooperation between autorickshaw and taxi drivers and traffic police, this chapter brings into view three interrelated concerns: (1) the gendered character of urban policing, (2) the emotional and moral ethos of urban law enforcement, and (3) the production of the city as a male space. Through these analyses, the chapter develops the concept of "homosocial trust" as an explanatory framework for understanding the gendered logic of cooperation between traffic police and transport workers through which urban mobility is governed and inhabited. The heuristic of "homosocial trust" captures the gendered structure of public morality and the logic of cooperation in everyday state practices by which the city is socially produced as a male space.

Controlling crime and maintaining order, key responsibilities of the urban police, proceed by identifying disruptive elements in the city. Practices of policing ascribe disrepute to particular people and places and hence are embedded in deeply ideological assumptions about who can legitimately exercise claim on state and community resources and who cannot (Fyfe 1995). The street thus emerges as a site of contestation between marginalized people and the police force. Urban researchers have demonstrated that working-class, racialized male youth are forced into situations of conflict with law enforcement officers over incongruent understandings of how the street ought to be inhabited (Cohen 1979; Anderson 1990; Fassin 2013). These studies have been important in underlining the role of policing practices in upholding urban inequalities.

Urban policing has followed a somewhat similar trajectory in India in the sense that law enforcement sustains the marginality of particular social groups in the city. Unemployed young men passing time in Meerut, for instance, are perceived as a threat to both morality and order maintenance and are subjected to police action under the guise of tackling sexual harassment in public spaces (Jeffrey 2010). Descriptions of the policing of sexual commerce in Mumbai note the use of physical force by the police on sex workers, who consider prostitutes to be sullying the respectability of middle-class people, even as they demand bribes from sex workers (Shah 2014). In the same city, following the communal riots of 1992–1993, policing in Muslim localities was intensified through more police stations than in non-Muslim neighborhoods (Blom Hansen 2001a). In New Delhi, residents of squatter settlements go to great lengths to acquaint themselves with the written law to avoid extortion from junior staff of the metropolitan police force (Datta 2012). However, given the blurred boundary between the Indian state and society at the local level (Gupta 1995), and the specificity of democratic processes in the region, the relationship between state functionaries and the urban poor plays out in ways that do not conform entirely to narratives of urban policing in northern cities. Discussions of the *tapori*, an urban male character peculiar to the subculture of twentieth-century Bombay who "stands at the intersection of morality and evil, between the legal and the illegal, between the world of work and those without work" (Mazumdar 2001, 4872), capture an aspect of the myriad ways in which the urban poor of India grapple with everyday policing. The tapori, by embodying the morality of the neighborhood, manages to hoodwink law through recourse to street cunning. These popular representations of everyday law in Hindi cinema highlight both the oppositional relations between the police and the marginalized and the common ground between them that opens avenues for the latter to negotiate with power in ways that enhance their right to the city.

Critical police studies—in India and internationally—has strived to reveal how law enforcement regulates the lives of marginalized publics. It is perhaps for this reason that issues of masculinity—inasmuch as masculinity is assumed to be a site of privilege rather than marginality—have largely been neglected in thinking about policing and city spaces. Thus, studies that underscore conflict between police and male youth in cities emphasize race, religion, and class relations and do not read it also as a reflex of gendered power. Feminist criminological research has sought to rectify this gender blindness by highlighting the influence of gender on crime and criminal justice systems. Some of the focus of these studies has been on the ways in which the police force, as a state institution, reflects and sustains dominant ideas of gender, including masculinity (Corsianos 2009; Silvestri 2017; Elski 2018). However, even as these studies read police culture through a gender lens, they do not consider in a sustained way the urban context in which much policing takes place. Indeed, it may be said that studies of policing that emphasize urbanity are neglectful of masculinity as an organizing principle, while those that are mindful of gender in police work seldom take into account how urbanism affects policing.

This chapter intervenes in this gap in thinking about urban policing. It does so by bringing police studies in dialogue with anthropological writings on the everyday state and masculinity in a way that emphasizes the everyday state's gender regime as a "structure of cathexis" (Connell 1990). For Connell, the Freudian idea of "cathexis" encapsulates the attachments of intimate relationships through which the gender order is maintained in societies. Following this use of the term, the discussion here unravels a set of emotional and moral evocations through which everyday state practices manufacture the gender order of the city. Such an approach draws thought to the vocabulary of masculinity used by men, who are otherwise framed in a conflictual relationship, to transact situational trust and make city streets inhabitable for themselves. It foregrounds mundane collaboration between state functionaries and marginal urban publics—alongside conflict—to highlight the masculinities of everyday state practice through which the city is reproduced as a space of patriarchal power. In doing so, the chapter highlights how everyday practices of urban policing manufacture the city as a male space by taking recourse to a particular moral vision of street and family life.

Laboring against Law

The police are always looking out to fine us. We want maximum passengers, so we would like to wait in all kinds of places. Police want to keep the roads clear for private cars. Our jobs are entirely different. Theirs is to push us along our way, ours is to wait on roads for passengers.
—Thirty-two-year-old auto driver

Transport vehicle operators' daily experiences on the road bear out the spatial constraints imposed by traffic law enforcement as it regulates mobility in the city. In Golpark, an upper-middle-class area in the city and a major crossroad, there are some fifty citations issued each day to transport workers. Some four thousand vehicles pass by this area each hour at peak times, approximately one thousand per hour in the afternoon. A crucial part of learning the ropes of transport labor is absorbing lessons about how to be safe from the reach of the law on city streets. This means cultivating alertness about the presence and methods of traffic police. Transport workers are therefore compelled to evolve what has been called, in the context of zero-tolerance policing in Los Angeles, "cop wisdom" (Stuart 2016), an interpretive schema that allows them to read and evade police interventions. Transport workers' interpretations of styles of traffic policing derive substantially from their reading of masculinity performances of particular officers. While hanging out at an autorickshaw depot, I heard drivers talk about a sergeant whom they perceived as harboring an arrogant pride about wielding the power of the uniform. The best way for autorickshaw drivers to deal with this officer, it emerged from their conversation, is to pretend to defer to his authority; such deference, it was thought, would stir a protective impulse toward those he has power over. A forty-six-year-old taxi driver explains how infrastructural elements of the vehicle are used to remain alert to the police presence on city streets: "If you are waiting to save five rupees on fuel, you are risking being fined for two hundred rupees. One has to be on the move continuously. If we wait, our attention is on the rear-view mirror. You have to run the moment you see police approaching. Like a goat in a butcher shop that has no guarantee when it will be killed. Our situation is like that with the police. Police have their strategy. They hide, away from the traffic signal, in some corner, on the lookout. Then they appear suddenly and fine you."

The bloody metaphor of butchering to delineate traffic law enforcement raises the question of precisely what is being denied life by the policing of urban public transport. Both traffic police and transport vehicle operators see themselves as facilitating everyday flows in the city. For transport workers to discharge this function in a way that is economically feasible, they need to save fuel costs by being stationary when they do not have passengers. There are insufficient bays for both taxis and autos, and hence parking is a major problem. Traffic laws make no concessions for inadequate parking space for public transport vehicles and keep operators on the move constantly. Hence, there is a firm conviction among transport workers that the laws and police officers are direct impediments to their profession and earnings. For transport workers, the presence of law enforcement officers, inasmuch as they obstruct the ability to approximate the male breadwinning role, is experienced as butchering the respectable breadwinning male. A twenty-seven-year-old taxi driver reasons, "Say I have parked the vehicle for a while. I know it is a no-parking zone, but what can I do, I need passengers! They will come harass us for this. I have to feed my family's stomach, so I will continue to break the law."

For working-class men systemically pitted against the law, the moral provocation for being their family's provider is much stronger than that of being a law-abiding urban subject. What is to be especially noted is that these two roles are repeatedly brought into conflict. An antithetical relationship—between the good urban citizen and the good family man—frames working-class men's inhabitation of city spaces: to be one, you have to forgo the other. The divergent pull of these two subject positions constitutes working-class men's ideas about security and risk in the urban outdoors. There is a collective belief among transport workers that they are routinely criminalized for acts that they undertake only to fulfill their duties as good family men. In being interpellated as likely lawbreakers as they go about their business, working-class men engaged in the informal urban economy are forced to justify their presence in the city. They have to continuously prove their innocence in the face of law. Anthropologists of the everyday state (Das 2004) have argued that the authority of laws often derives from beyond written rules. The accounts that public transport workers provide of their encounters with traffic law enforcement suggest that patriarchal scripts of masculinity embolden men to question the authority of law and justify their efforts to circumvent it. Male transport workers' efforts to build a case for their innocence, in response to legal and social opprobrium, take recourse to the moral value attached to the breadwinner ideal of hegemonic masculinity: "Once I was waiting for passengers in a no-parking zone. A sergeant came up to me and asked for my papers. I didn't have them right then. He said he would arrest me and lock up my car. I told him, 'Sir, I am not a thug, I'm not a thief. I am just trying to earn some money to feed my family. I am at fault but I am not a criminal'" (twenty-eight-year-old auto driver).

Seen in terms of existing traffic laws, in this instance the driver is guilty of two offences: Rule 126, disallowing the vehicle to be stationary at a public space, which carries a fine of INR100 for the first violation, and nonproduction of certificates (Rule 158[1]), which carries a fine of INR100 for the first infringement. But we see the policeman threatening the driver with Rule 207, which empowers officers to detain vehicles if the driver is unable to produce proper documentation. In their encounters with traffic police, transport workers make a moral distinction between the lawbreaker and the criminal. While the criminal's unlawful behavior stems from moral turpitude or greed, the lawbreaker oversteps legal directives only to be a provider for his family and hence deserves lenience. Transport vehicle operators' need to separate the lawbreaker from the criminal captures the working-class male's use of moral reasoning to refuse the delegitimization of his labor in the city. The moral logic by which they claim pardon for breaking traffic rules draws on a shared consensus about the role of familial masculinity. Indeed, one of the ways in which transport workers cooperate with traffic police to claim a right to labor in the city—as we will see in more detail below—is to make use of the discourse of male breadwinning, which has considerable resonance with male law enforcement officers. In inhabiting the city as workers in the informal economy, working-class men wrestle against two kinds of failures—the failure to be good men (for being unable to earn sufficiently) and the failure to be good urban subjects (for not abiding by the law). The disciplinary presence of traffic law enforcement on city streets is experienced by transport workers as a major provocation for both these forms of failure.

Both taxi and autorickshaw drivers consider the workings of traffic law to be whimsical, entirely reliant on the caprice of individual police officers. They are unable to fully understand which driving practice will provoke police intervention and which will not. Traffic police may turn a blind eye to a particular action on one day, only to impose strict penalties the following day. It has been argued that the state's rules and regulations may be illegible not only to the poor because of low levels of literacy but often also to those who are responsible for implementing state rules (Das 2004). My ethnography showed that even officers find it difficult to keep up with new police orders that alter the tenets of lawful driving in the city. This confusion coexists with the impulse of traffic police to make a masculine display of their power to direct mobility on city streets. As a forty-one-year-old taxi operator told me, "It's as though they stop us when they are in the mood to have *khaini* [chewing tobacco]. They call us, ask for *khaini*. Then, with a look of relish on their faces, they will ask us to go, saying—'I would have fined you, but you seem like a nice guy so I won't. Now go!'"

Experienced vehicle operators are able to identify a semblance of logic behind apparently random ticketing—what police studies scholars call "ideal economy of intervention" (Bittner 1967)—by identifying personality traits of particular officers. Here, the sociability among transport workers and with traffic officials allows drivers to collectively identify patterns in police actions. Thus, anecdotes about specific traffic personnel and their own interactions enable drivers to discern which strategy to use to secure leniency. With some traffic policemen, humor might be the best approach, whereas for others pleading may yield better results; with yet others, it may be best to simply be silent and deferential so as to be let off with the smallest penalty.

Law enforcement officers question not only transport workers' right to the city but also their sense of ownership over their vehicles. While the interiors of most autorickshaws are sparse, others are elaborately decorated with flowers, stereo systems, showpieces, tassels, and religious objects. A thirty-eight-year-old auto operator told me that his vehicle used to be done up but he had the décor taken down because the police started regularly fining him for it:

"Many drivers like decorating their cars. It's a simple wish. But they are not allowed. The police say, 'What is all this, why have you made the vehicle into a bar?' I had some flowers here. One policeman stopped and asked me to take them down. I said, 'What problem are these creating for anyone?' Still he gave me a case for three hundred rupees. Police really torture us."

Ulf Mellström (2004) has drawn attention to the centrality of technology in men's lives and argued that this relationship be understood through the analytical tropes of power and pleasure embedded in the process of handling artifacts. Transport workers' narratives emphasize the impediments that traffic law enforcement introduces to drivers feeling empowered by their machines and deriving pleasure from them. Legal injunctions that forbid vehicular decorations and playing music and the lack of property rights collude with the moralism of police officers regarding entertainment and alcohol—"why have you made the vehicle into a bar?"—to disrupt any desire in drivers to forge a connection with the vehicles they spend countless working hours in. For these reasons, even though the vehicle in abstraction is an important component of drivers' work-based identity, most drivers do not forge an attachment to their vehicles.

Social Difference

For transport workers, moving through the city is an unceasing effort to escape the reach of law. There is no one way in which drivers respond to the persecuting presence of law in their working lives, as different situations call forth different strategies of coping. While there is a general feeling among most transport workers that the law is against them, there is also a sense that law enforcement officers discriminate between different social groups. A forty-three-year-old Hindu Bengali auto driver believes, "In the Park Circus route drivers drive very recklessly. There the police does not dare to tell them too much. They have an understanding. They have a monthly arrangement. It is a *Mohammedan* area."

If many Hindu drivers reinforce the Islamophobic notion that the police fear a Muslim masculinity that is prone to recklessness and violence, many Muslim drivers feel unduly persecuted because of their religion. A number of drivers complained that they are unable to observe *roza* because of the demanding nature of their job. Not following religious tenets often incites feelings of guilt. They are unable to read *namaz* largely because of the legal compulsion to be on the move. A twenty-seven-year-old Muslim auto driver who operates in the Park Circus area noted, "In other localities things are not so bad. Here the idea is to keep these people under pressure. You learn to handle that pressure with experience. Police think this is a Muslim guy, so let's fine him more. They ask for our names. Those with Hindu names are given a lower fine. The police who are Muslim themselves understand our situation somewhat. But they are few."

My interactions with law enforcement officers showed that most endorse this discriminatory view of Muslim masculinity as particularly predisposed to lawlessness. While few police officers admitted to it openly, I did get a sense while speaking to them that they believe Muslim drivers to be more of a threat to public order than drivers of any other faith. Some reasoned that this has to do not with religion but with the low levels of education and social awareness that prevail among Muslims. Such a language of police assessment reflects the shift identified by Thomas Blom Hansen (2001a), in the context of policing in Mumbai, from a "vulgar sociology" of the Muslim hooligan into a simplistic "sociology of Muslims" that reproduces stereotypes about the community. It is also worth pointing out that the Muslim neighborhoods in which I conducted fieldwork—Park Circus and Tiljala—besides being associated with petty criminality and lawlessness, are also identified by police as localities harboring terrorists in the city (Chatterjee 2017). As a result, slum dwellers in these neighborhoods—of which Muslim transport workers are a part—are regularly subjected to police scrutiny. However, if religion differentiates working-class men's encounters with police officers, it does not necessarily lend homogeneity to Muslim transport workers' experiences of law. Some may indeed use the legal establishment selectively to manufacture prestige among other men within their community. A thirty-four-year-old Muslim auto-operator recalled with considerable relish, "Once I found a driver from another route nearby, driving in our route. I immediately reported him to the police. After that all the guys in this route recognize me, they respect me. They say that guy lives on his own mettle."

While the presence of the state is largely experienced by transport workers as a restriction, state functionaries may also be treated as a resource for claiming territorial rights in the neighborhood. Such honor contests notwithstanding, common experiences of marginality at the hands of traffic law enforcement usually make it possible for transport workers to forge a sense of solidarity across community differences. Bihari taxi operators, for instance, feel especially persecuted by police on account of their immigrant status in the city. Many explained that because they typically have lower levels of literacy than Bengali drivers, traffic officials exploit their poor understanding of important documents such as pollution and tax papers. A thirty-five-year-old Hindu Bengali auto driver recounted,

> The police constantly trouble taxi drivers. We see it happening right in front of our eyes. We can see clearly as we wait in the auto stand. For no good reason they will stop taxis, especially if the drivers are Hindustani. They will be told that some senior officer is calling them. The driver will plead. This is the arrangement—either you pay one hundred rupees to the tea stall owner, to be collected by the police later, or they lodge a case of five hundred rupees right then. The driver has no choice but to keep one hundred rupees at the tea stall. The police don't take the money directly anymore because there are cameras now.

Different forms of transport in the city throw up distinct challenges for transport workers. Despite these differences, men operating one mode of transport are able to recognize forms of marginalization that those operating another kind of public vehicle are subjected to by both the general public and law enforcement. Transport workers harbor an understanding of the law that recognizes both the specific experiences of particular social groups—in this case, the vulnerability of Bihari migrants—as well as the general marginalization that affects them collectively. This account also demonstrates how police officers may circumvent CCTV and body camera surveillance, which has been introduced. Such "folklore of corruption" (Verma 1999) about traffic law enforcement has a paradoxical role in framing relations between different groups of transport workers, both producing factions among them (for example, when they sense differential treatment) and endowing a commonality of urban experience with respect to the everyday state.

Camaraderie

Notwithstanding the considerable disaffection that transport workers express toward the police, there exists a measure of mutual understanding between these groups. This understanding between men stems from shared notions about both masculinity and its relation to urban life. A thirty-seven-year-old traffic sergeant said, "The thing with auto drivers is that they are mostly local boys. They have lived in this locality all their lives. So they take liberties thinking this is their area and no one will tell them anything here. There are drivers who will tell us, 'Sir you are fining us here; we have grown up here, we used to swim in ponds here as kids, play football in the fields. Don't fine us here.'"

Autorickshaw operators display what might be termed "neighborhood masculinity" in the course of their daily mobilities in the city. As we have seen in an earlier chapter, in Kolkata they traverse the same route within neighborhoods in which they usually live. This spatial familiarity produces a form of masculinity that expresses a sense of entitlement to absolute freedom within the neighborhood. By dint of having grown up in the locality, men seem to expect unfettered sanction—both social and legal—for

their usage of neighborhood space. Working-class masculinity has a specific relation to the street. The high density within the slums in which they reside forces poor male youth onto public space, especially interior lanes of neighborhoods, as a zone of sociability. In Kolkata, boys' clubs—where young working-class men congregate to play indoor games, watch television, and even sleep at night if there is no space for them in their homes—are ubiquitous in neighborhoods and have a distinct social history. In the course of its thirty-four years of rule, the left-front government in West Bengal used these male spaces for political recruitment through its patronage system. They occupy a morally ambiguous place, associated with idleness and vice on the one hand, but also are seen as part of the associational life of the neighborhood through the support these clubs sometimes render in community affairs (Gooptu 2007). Autorickshaw operators are a part of this habitus. A twenty-eight-year-old police officer captured the pulse of the neighborhood masculinity of autorickshaw drivers when he said, "They take liberties in their own localities. This is the nature of this city. Everyone is a hero in his own locality." For working-class men, the feeling of entitlement embedded in neighborhood masculinity is also a desire for legitimacy in rapidly gentrifying neighborhoods that are pushing them to their fringes. Law enforcement personnel are aware of this and, to some degree, are sympathetic to these male claims on neighborhood space. Such camaraderie demonstrates the extent to which legal regulation of urban traffic is inflected by shared assumptions of class, space, and gender between men.

Auto drivers' circular mobility and the particular form of masculinity that this enables lead to a kind of sociability with law enforcement. As a forty-five-year-old police officer explains,

> We certainly get to know auto drivers over time. I not only remember their faces and names but also some details about their lives. Some faces become familiar because they are regular offenders. We will tell them, "Arindam, again you are making the same mistake? How many times will you get fined for the same offence?" His father was very ill and hospitalized. On his way to seeing him, he would tell me the status of his father's health. Then one day I saw him in a *kacha* [mourning clothes], so I asked him if everyone else in the family is alright.

Interactions of this nature through which officers get familiar with the personal biographies of autorickshaw operators are largely absent in taxi drivers' accounts of their encounters with the police. Interpersonal knowledge flows between police and auto operators allow some degree of mutual appreciation to evolve between them and create an opening for indulgences to be sought and granted. Police officers are entrusted with the responsibility of implementing state rules, but they are simultaneously embedded in local worlds and their habitats (Das 2004). Indeed, officers endorse, to some extent, the spatial claims of neighborhood masculinity inasmuch as they too share the male sense of entitlement about urban space with respect to neighborhoods they identify as their own. In their conversations with me, traffic police—especially those in the lower ranks—naturalized working-class men's sense of entitlement to neighborhood space, using the importance of particular urban localities to their biographies to legitimize these claims. Cooperation and understanding proceed from the shared social backgrounds of some police officers and drivers. A forty-year-old traffic official who spent his formative years in a small village in West Bengal recounted,

> I am not used to speaking to women too much. So I hesitate to offer help to women. I remember this one time when I went out of my way to offer help to a middle-aged woman who I thought was struggling on the road. She reacted very rudely to me, as though I had misbehaved with her simply by speaking to her. I felt terribly judged. I see some taxi drivers from Bihar having the same problem. We don't know how to speak to city women and they don't like us very much. We are not up to their standard.

Police constables occupying the lowest ranks in the police force and transport workers sometimes inhabit similar social worlds. As Fuller and Harris (2001, 15) write, "[The state's] lower echelons at least are always staffed by people with whom some kind of social relationship can or could exist . . . the boundary between state and society . . . is . . . negotiable according to social context and position." It is important to underline the commonalities of male experience in the city—in addition to those of class—that help forge a sliver of understanding between men otherwise placed in hierarchical relation to one another. In this instance we see how a traffic official's recognition of his insertion in a rural gender regime that hinders easy cross-gender interactions impels identification with other men who share this version of masculinity, one that is hesitant to communicate with unfamiliar women in the city. This idea of a nonurban masculinity that is devalued by the cultural ideals of city life is also produced by a shared experience of some urban middle-class women's contempt for rural men.

Cooperation between state actors and transport workers stems also from police officers' acknowledgment that fearing the law does not necessarily lead to lawful actions. Many spoke of using familiarity with transport workers to improve civic knowledge among them: "We need to tell them that the policeman is your friend. The thought is imbibed in us that we need to fear the police. This fear needs to go for real cooperation to happen on the roads. These channels of communication need to be created. Imperialist era of policing, traces of that are still there. That needs to go."

The discursive positioning of traffic policemen as friends of transport workers captures homosocial intimacy as a mode of governing public transport in the city. It opens an avenue for police officers to use male camaraderie to conditionally befriend transport workers, signaling the malleability of the everyday state to practice different styles of gender as it regulates urban spaces. Again, personal contact is far easier established with autorickshaw drivers, on account of their circumscribed geographies, than with taxi drivers who are a more itinerant lot. Such forms of communication might have been initiated to impose the state will on city streets with greater effect, but transport workers are able to use this familiarity to maneuver around police intervention. Fleeting conviviality allows transport workers to anticipate the logic of police intervention. There are, of course, clear limits to the familiarity that can be established between transport workers and law enforcement officers, as conveyed by this metaphorical line that repeatedly arose in my conversations with public transport vehicle drivers: "If the horse [police] becomes friendly with the grass [transport workers], he won't be able to eat." Traffic policemen also confirm the limits to camaraderie with drivers: "Being friendly with drivers helps us to explain the law to them. But I would never be friends with them, have tea or snacks with them as I am having with you. If I do that they will no longer respect my uniform. I won't be able to do my job as a policeman" (forty-three-year-old police officer).

Even as traffic policemen regard transport workers as a menace to order maintenance in city streets, they simultaneously consider them to be a vital infrastructure of support for the police, particularly for discharging public welfare in the city. A thirty-nine-year-old traffic sergeant says, "There is no question that many auto and taxi drivers are very helpful. If there are accidents on the road the man in the suit will pass by in his car without stopping. But the drivers will take the injured to the hospital. In my thirteen years as a traffic police, I have seen this many times." In the absence of reliable emergency services, the network of transport workers—specifically taxi and autorickshaw operators—are called upon to render situational support in times of urgent mishap. If, as Jane Jacobs famously argued, "eyes on the street" play a significant role in creating public safety through informal surveillance, transport workers in the city often function as the hands of the road, providing assistance in difficult situations on city streets well beyond the call of their profession. A traffic constable shared with me an anecdote about how after a fierce storm a fallen tree had blocked a major connecting road; a group of auto drivers got together and had it cleared without waiting for municipal services to handle the problem. Another police officer narrated an instance of support: "Just yesterday two women came to me in tears and said they have both been pickpocketed in a bus. I asked an auto driver I knew to take them to the police station to lodge a complaint and then to drop them home. I gave the driver the fare. Several drivers help us out in this way."

Those who occupy the margins of the state use ideas of gift and sacrifice to situate state apparatuses as marginal to the citizen-body (Das 2004). By functioning as an informal infrastructure of support on city streets, transport workers position themselves as a resource for managing urban unpredictability and find a legitimizing ground for laboring in the city. In this way, the state's inability to fulfill its welfare role is seized by public transport workers as an opportunity to lend credence to their right to the city.

Heteronormativity

A key instrument of the Safe Drive Save Life program—detailed earlier—is regular sensitization workshops with public transport workers in the city. The workshops, conducted in the afternoons to make use of lean traffic times, take the form of a classroom setting. Transport vehicle operators gather in a room fitted with a whiteboard and audiovisual aids, as sergeants take them through the key learning points of the day. A range of promotional material from the campaign adorns the classroom walls: a prominent poster announces grandly, "In my enlightenment are the seeds of a new city," hinting at the codes of conduct that get characterized as informed civic actions on city streets. Pamphlets and other written documents are not circulated in these workshops because most transport workers either are nonliterate or have low levels of literacy. Drivers are informally urged to attend these workshops. Traffic constables cajole transport workers they meet on the road; an official invitation is sent to transport unions to send drivers to these events regularly. Drivers who successfully complete these workshops are issued cards bearing the title "Enlightened Driver"; this is a way of incentivizing participation and gradually making attendance compulsory. Workshop facilitators stress that following laws means less fines, which means more earnings for transport workers.

As we wait for class to begin one summer afternoon—which usually has the strength of about fifteen participants—many drivers attend to calls on their mobile phones. Some complain of being trapped, while others report with a distinct ring of pride in their voice, "I am attending class." A few of them gather around a smartphone and start watching educational videos uploaded by the Kolkata traffic police on YouTube. Today's workshop facilitator is a twenty-nine-year-old traffic sergeant who has been on the road for about two years. He begins the day's proceedings by sharing a statistic: "Road accident deaths in India are among the highest in the world and 90 percent of the times the cause is negligent driving. We have to reduce accidents. The problem is that the level of knowledge among drivers is very low. We all know how driver's licenses are released in this country. Let's both keep it a secret for now."

To address this problem of inadequate civic knowledge, a large component of these workshops is devoted to sharing information about traffic laws, especially those pertaining to public transport vehicles. Considerable time is spent discussing CCTV footage of road accidents to identify the cause and how they can be avoided. There are discussions of speeding, with workshop facilitators gently chiding drivers for their bravado. The facilitator's strategy also includes showing images of drivers helping the public, with the objective to reinforce positive behavior in public spaces. This all-male environment of teaching and learning how to navigate mobility lawfully in the city is powerfully conditioned by a shared culture of heterosexual urban masculinity. Law enforcement officers' and transport workers' insertion into the gender regime of heteronormative masculinity shapes the diagnosis of and proposed solutions to problems of risk/safety and good/bad conduct in the city. As the twenty-nine-year-old sergeant explained in class that afternoon, "It's alright that you [autorickshaw driver] are asking women to sit in front, next to you. The smell of her perfume, her shampooed hair blowing in your face, we all enjoy these things. But also ask her to hold on to the auto's railing properly."

Research on male homosocial bonding (Bird 1996; Flood 2008) underscores sexual storytelling and competitive sex talk as the primary performative tropes of heterosexual masculinity in same-sex settings. The structural imbalance of power between male police officers and male transport workers and the formal context of the classroom usually disallow overtly salacious conversations, which are common in men's friendships. Nevertheless, their interactions and the urban narratives these exchanges shore up are structured by ideologies of heteronormative masculinity and desire. Law enforcement officers' efforts to popularize safe driving practices often rest on the naturalization of male heterosexual lust in public space. In the fieldwork note above, the young male police officer presents a particularly sensual image—invoking olfactory and tactile sensations—to weld heterosexual urban erotics with steering habits that can minimize the risk of road accidents. The particular workshop proceedings I have been reporting on concluded with the sergeant reminding transport workers, "Drive properly not out of fear of the police but for your own self; if your license is confiscated for three months, how will your family eat?"

Transport workers are persuaded to follow traffic norms and safe driving techniques so that they will be able to fulfill their provider roles as men. Order maintenance in public spaces is therefore tied to the performance of an exalted version of patriarchal masculinity in the home. State actors and transport vehicle operators coproduce the masculinization of public spaces in the sense that heteropatriarchal conceptions of men's social roles provide the vocabulary and interpretive framework for understanding public safety and order on city streets. In Kolkata, these conceptions of gender roles are embedded in a particular contextualized form of middle-class, upper-caste Bengali patriarchy, one that ideologically ties respectable femininity to domesticity and, parallelly, the capacity to provide such "protection" to women to a valued index of masculinity (Ray 2000). Conversely, the inability to keep women in the home, especially on account of men's inability to provide adequately, is seen as a failure of masculinity. For Bihari taxi drivers in Kolkata, sending adequate remittances back to their villages is a key achievement of masculinity in a social context where widespread male out-migration from rural Bihar has led to married women assuming a greater role in decision making and household financial management and increased participation in the public sphere (Datta and Mishra 2011).

The imbrication of traffic law enforcement with the ideals of heteronormative masculinity ought not to be seen as a strategic expression of state rationality. Patriarchal ideas of masculinity are not deployed by policemen in an instrumental way to manage traffic problems. Rather, everyday practices of mobility and law regulation on city streets proceed through mutual obeisance to cultural norms and ideals of masculinity that link lawful conduct in public to the performance of idealized gender roles in private. A traffic sergeant, forty-two years of age, who often leads such workshops, recounted, "In the first phase we ask about drivers' lifestyle, family members, what his burdens are. Their attitudes on the street are dependent on this, so it is important for us to know. We try to address these. If his father is ill, we try to get a doctor to see him. If his children can't buy books for school, any father will be troubled. We put them in touch with NGOs that give out free books. Problems in the home are expressed outside."

Law enforcement officers' diagnosis of the problem of unruly driving practices presumes a close connection between the intimate sphere of family life and the wider interaction order of public spaces. They suggest, in fact, a reversal of the more common understanding of men resolving troubles in the public domain by taking it out on the family. Officers' view that the stability of the public order is reliant on the stability of family life authorizes gender roles that reinforce sexual division of labor. In other words, law enforcement personnel psychologize men's unruly behavior on city streets by connecting it to the instability of the patriarchal family. In the terms of this discourse of traffic law enforcement, securing the city from reckless driving entails safeguarding male power in the family. The governance of urban traffic simultaneously constitutes the home and the city as spaces of male authority.

Moral tropes of good fathering routinely emerge as policing tactics that shame drivers for particular kinds of behavior on roads. I encountered, for instance, a police officer chastising an auto driver for using abusive language toward a passenger, saying that his daughter would be ashamed of him if she heard him speak like this. The social life of the autorickshaw, as we have seen, allows such biographical information to circulate; the manner in which it seeps into traffic policing captures the structuring influence of heteronormative masculinity on the everyday work of law in the city. A recent billboard advertisement for the Kolkata Traffic Police shows a montage of two images of a man riding a bike with a boy seated in front; the boy in the first image—titled "Daddy Fool"— is not wearing a helmet, while the second—titled "Daddy Cool"— shows the boy wearing one. In the traffic training workshops, transport workers are routinely shown videos of accidents not merely to identify the causes—for instance, a taxi violates a traffic signal and is mowed down by a truck—but also to show the consequences of recklessness on drivers' families. Participants hear stories of families engulfed by poverty after the death/disability of a transport worker due to deviant driving. The failure to approximate men's provider role, to be good sons/husbands/fathers, is held out to transport vehicle operators as a major consequence of lawlessness and as a deterrent to risky driving. Transport workers also read traffic officers through the lens of men's provider role. While traveling in a taxi in the course of my fieldwork, I heard the driver tell an adjacent taxi operator as both vehicles waited at a traffic signal that a new sergeant who is in charge of that area seems better than the others because he understands how difficult it is for migrant taxi drivers to financially support their families. The other driver responded that the police ought to empathize with them for the burdens they shoulder for the sake of their families back in their villages. The general cynicism toward law enforcement personnel notwithstanding, several transport operators also noted the long chain of command in which traffic police officers are placed. A thirty-six-year-old taxi driver reasons, "They also have pressure on them. We have heard and seen. On the wireless phone, as they are giving us a case, some DC [deputy commissioner] is telling them, 'File twenty cases every day otherwise your job is on the line.' So they also have pressure. We have noticed we are fined more toward the end of every month. They also have families to feed. Everyone is under pressure in this city."

Men's mutual recognition of the pressures of working life draws attention to the homosociality of public spaces, which is one of the principal ideological tropes by which the everyday state produces the city as masculine and inimical to the presence of women. Several traffic policemen confess that if they followed the rule book to the letter, the sheer volume of fines would make it impossible for transport workers to provide for their families. Thus, they mostly enforce the more serious offences (such as drunken driving, speeding, running red lights) and indulge the minor ones (changing lanes, overtaking). In this way, the policing of urban traffic and the functioning of the everyday state in the city are mediated by the heteronormative construction of paid work as the primary site of adult masculine identity.

The modern city is inherently uncertain in the sense that the unknown and the unmanageable are constitutive of urban life (Zeiderman et al. 2015). One aspect of this urban unpredictability is the work of law enforcement in cities, especially for the urban poor. Suspicion being the fulcrum of policing, the uncertainty intrinsic to any suspicious response to a person or situation is what occupies the gap between codified law and its application (Asad 2004). Those laboring on the urban margins must find ways of surviving both the general uncertainty of urban life and the particular visage that this arbitrariness assumes in the form of policing. Consequently, "improvised lives" in cities of the Global South depend variously on an economy of reciprocity, manipulation, and trust (Simone 2019). Such relations of trust between strangers in the city are not an automatic product of simply being together in the same place but the outcome of everyday urban practice (Amin 2012).

The interactions described in this chapter suggest that law enforcement in the city is fundamentally inflected by the value-laden associations between masculinity and the sociability of urban life. Men's sense of ownership over urban space as a site of leisure and work impinges on everyday practices of law on city streets. These interactions also suggest that heteronormative formations of masculinity, especially idealized gender roles within the family, calibrate how the everyday state governs urban mobility. Patriarchal tropes of the good father and the responsible family man and the naturalization of male heterosexual desire suture cooperative relations between urban actors that law enforcement participates in. These gendered figures, which feature prominently in policing practices in the city, form the basis for a feminist framework to understand how the city sustains male privilege and the role of everyday cooperation in the sustenance of inequality in cities. To elaborate, I lay out the concept of "homosocial trust" as a heuristic for tracking the cooperative gestures and moral inflections of the everyday state through which the patriarchal city is reproduced.

The idea of "homosociality," while an important one in masculinity studies, has seldom been invoked in scholarship on urban life. In masculinity studies, the term is defined as social bonds between people of the same sex and is typically used to demonstrate how sociabilities between men sustain patriarchal social orders, particularly through the defense of hegemonic ideals of masculinity (Hammarén and Johansson 2014). In other words, friendly bonds through which men establish horizontal relationships among themselves function to strengthen hierarchical gender norms. Recent reformulations of the term, however, have critiqued this use as too deterministic, which forecloses the possibility that some forms of homosocial bonding between men may recast patriarchal masculinities along more egalitarian lines (Hammarén and Johansson 2020). "Trust" has been defined as the openness of a social actor to be vulnerable to another social entity (be it a person, social group, or institution) with the expectation that they will safeguard the welfare of the trusting person (Schilke, Reimann, and Cook 2021). It is understood as a situation in which one can expect favorable reactions from people and/or institutions. The reward of trust is that it reduces the contingencies of social life by establishing generalizable patterns in how people, places, and institutions operate (Möllering 2001). Despite conflictual relations between transport workers and traffic police, there is a measure of reliance between these groups of men as they move through city spaces. This mutual reliance between hierarchically positioned men, who are situated variously in the state apparatus and on the urban margins, is what I am calling "homosocial trust."

Urban living—and encounters with law enforcement—is replete with the onslaught of the unexpected (Amin 2012). Consequently, managing the inherent unpredictability of the city—and the whimsy of urban policing—demands practicing trust in social situations (Blokland 2017). The need to trust arises from the pervasiveness of urban uncertainty. But how is trust produced in the everyday city? The cultivation of trust depends on the moral orientation of the other, that they will do what is morally right in a given situation. Trust in the other's moral goodness develops through repeated encounters in which the other acts as is morally expected. Homosocial trust as a heuristic helps to recognize the moral vocabulary of masculinity that enables men to transact situational forms of support and manage both the caprice of law and the uncertainty of city life. Such trust is homosocial in that it is predicated on men's mutual recognition of the morally exalted status of male breadwinning, the city as the primary site for this achievement of masculinity, and social compulsions of men's roles as members of the heteronormative family. Police work is not simply about following the rule books to the letter; there are also other social norms that authorize some policing practices while discrediting others. Homosocial trust between men is a major structuring principle of the everyday work of urban law enforcement: it guides tacit notions of what composes "good" police work and what falls under "bad" policing practices and opens avenues for marginalized men to negotiate sanctioned modes of laboring and being in city spaces. Public transport workers, in inhabiting the urban informal economy, are unable to repose "procedural trust" (Sztompka 1999)—the faith that people invest in formal institutions and institutional procedures—in traffic law enforcement. Rather, their relationship with police officers is framed by mutual suspicion and entails a continuous negotiation with unpredictability. However, the fundamental uncertainty of urban life encapsulates law enforcement officers as well; they too need to minimize the contingencies of living and working in the city. The scripts of homosociality provide a powerful basis for traffic police work and cultivating trust with other men laboring in the urban outdoors. A forty-one-year-old university-educated traffic sergeant recounts,

> I remember in the peak of summer, some six years ago, I was on duty. Suddenly I blacked out. The road pitch was so hot my skin was burnt. Some taxi drivers nearby took me to the hospital.

They guarded my motorbike so that no one could touch it. They bore the entire money for this initial phase. They reported the incident to the police station. When I tried to return the money they would not accept it. They said they don't want the money because they have noticed that I understand the pressures these drivers are under. I am concerned about their families, their children's well-being. They did this so that I could also return to my wife and child. For me, this is what makes Kolkata a living city.

Homosocial trust between men, which is premised on a shared moral investment in patriarchal ideals of masculinity, is a way of tiding over unexpected dangers of city life and the suspicious gaze of law enforcement. Thus, when the group of taxi drivers refuses to accept money for the help they extended to the policeman suddenly taken ill, they do so by morally exalting the patriarchal association between waged work and adult familial masculinity. Such gestures of kindness between men in the city carry with them a moral expectation of reciprocity: that their burdens of breadwinner masculinity, their familial roles as son, husbands, and fathers, will be acknowledged just as they recognize this struggle in other men's urban lives. Through such moral reasoning, male homosocial bonding patterns interactions on city streets and enables men to identify and trust sources of support amid the vagaries of city living. Homosocial trust between men in the context of law enforcement reproduces the city as a patriarchal space in the sense that the moral terrain of heteronormative masculinity shapes the ordering function of the everyday state. In several interactions with law enforcement, this collective male assumption about the inherent moral value of hegemonic forms of masculinity emerges as the main provenance of judgment. The folk criminology of traffic officials to adjudicate between which offence requires intervention, to what degree, and which can be overlooked derives from this homosocial culture of trust between men on city streets. The figure of the responsible family man who labors in the city and the normative association between men's leisure and urban spaces mediate transport vehicle operators' requests for leniency from law enforcement and also make the fickleness of policing practices partially intelligible. Such metaphors and practices of masculinity through which homosocial trust between men is transacted are intrinsic to the gender regime of the everyday state and the normative production of the city as a community of men.

Conclusion

The relationship between urban policing and the disenfranchised has been understood primarily through the lens of social conflict. Recent ethnographies of the everyday state have conceptualized it as constitutively ambivalent and the police as simultaneously enforcing laws and partnering with criminal activities. These studies have shown how the police's selective "collusion" with unlawful practices maintains the illegal status of marginal urban subjects (Auyero and Sobering 2019). The narratives recorded in this chapter convey the logics of masculinity that underlie such conflict while also enabling cooperation and trust between police and drivers. The disciplinary presence of traffic police is perceived to prompt two opposing pulls on transport workers: the failure to be good men through providing for their families and the failure to be good urban subjects by abiding the law. Traffic norms demand obedience from transport vehicle operators, but observing these rules fully would mean censure for failing to provide adequately for their families. Much of the friction between traffic police and public transport workers stems from this opposition.

Surviving the city, however, requires traffic police and public transport drivers to also collaborate. Such cooperation is premised on and strengthens the associations between men and the urban outdoors as legitimate sites of male labor and leisure. The grammar of situational forms of trust draws on heteronormative valuations of masculinity—such as the exalted figure of the good father, the responsible family man, the naturalization of heterosexual desire—and its associations with urban spaces. Such modes of cooperation between unequal men serve to make the city inhabitable for the marginalized but also sustain it as a space of male privilege relative to women. If studies of urban policing have shown how conflict between law enforcement personnel and the marginalized sustains urban inequalities, this chapter has shown the part played by trust in reproducing gender inequalities in the city and the vocabulary of masculinity by which such trust is negotiated.

The heuristic of "homosocial trust" brings into view some gendered features of the everyday state in city spaces: state-society interactions in the city partially rest on situational trust that is evolved in mundane urban encounters with law enforcement; hegemonic metaphors of masculinity supply the terms by which such trust is enacted; the persuasive power of such metaphors that characterize police work in the city is to be explained by the moral force of gendered ideas about urban uncertainty, fickleness of law, masculinity, family, and the associational life of neighborhoods. Moral discourses of masculinity, camaraderie between men, and the spatial bases of gendered identity constitute the ground for state functionaries and the urban majority to cooperate and forge situational trust in the uncertain city. For Simmel (1990, 318, 178), "without the general trust that people have in each other, society itself would disintegrate." Quotidian interactions between traffic police and drivers in the circuits of public transportation convey the spatial imperatives of masculinity through which trust is produced in the city and its part in maintaining the gendered urban social fabric. Relations of trust between strangers that are based on moral reasonings that legitimize the city as a site of hegemonic masculine performances simultaneously heighten women's sense of being out of place in the outdoors and embolden ideological structures that hinder women's access to public spaces. The emphasis on trust and collaboration in practices of law enforcement, therefore, far from eschewing a focus on urban inequalities, draws thought to the gendered moral vocabulary through which urban policing produces and maintains the everyday city as a space of patriarchal power.

5

City Characters

Morality

A migrant taxi driver who would occasionally buy sex from sex workers in Kolkata decides to stop after he has children. An ethical discourse that ties responsible fatherhood to proper sexual conduct and a conception of sin that perpetuates from parent to child influence his sexual choices in the city. A police officer chastises an autorickshaw driver for using abusive language toward a passenger, saying that his daughter would be ashamed of him if she heard him speak in this manner; this is no way for a good father to behave on city streets. An autorickshaw driver is morally repulsed by stories of transport workers sexually assaulting women; he explains that being a transport worker is a noble profession because it entails providing public service to urban dwellers. In his narrative, male sexual violence is discouraged by an ethic of public good that normatively frames transport work in the city.

An undertone of several of the gendered encounters described in this book is a set of moral orientations between transport workers, traffic personnel, and passengers. This chapter isolates some of these urban moments to draw thought to the moral making of a city of men. To think of the city as an interactional space is to ask what propels urban residents' orientations toward each other. The interactions that inhere in the mobile routines of public transportation are workshops where urban dwellers cultivate and perform ethical personhoods. Copresence in transit systems is negotiated by assuming distinctly moral positions about conduct in the city. To make sense of the problems and opportunities of daily mobilities, urbanites attach moral values to people and places. And it is through the ascription of moral meanings to everyday urban happenings that the city and its residents come into being. The social reproduction of the patriarchal city as a community of men depends on everyday moral judgments and practices. Through the exercise of such ordinary moral assessments, a crew of urban characters appear in the spaces of public transportation in the city. These city characters capture the moral values through which everyday interactions in mobility spaces become sociologically meaningful.

Everyday Morality

For instance, middle-class suspicions about the urban poor, especially their readiness to impute extractive intentions to the working class, often obstruct kindly gestures from transport workers. When acts of goodness from drivers, such as helping a waylaid passenger to reach their destination as conveniently as possible, are misread by passengers as deceitful, such reactions compel transport workers to reconsider their intent to do good. The middle-class passenger's urgency to be street smart, to not be hoodwinked by drivers, clashes with the moral intentions of the urban poor to be helpful. Such thwarted recognition of the urban poor's ethical impulse significantly depletes the quality of urban life for the working class. Transport workers register great frustration at their ethical conduct being repeatedly misread as dishonest. In fact, they want their kindness to be acknowledged by passengers and characterize acts of goodness as futile if they pass unnoticed or are misconstrued as exploitative. As a gesture of kindly indulgence, autorickshaw drivers may allow a mother traveling with a young child to pay only for the adult; but drivers become reluctant to do good when such offers go unacknowledged. From such omissions, the figure of the ungrateful passenger arises, and by extension an everyday urban calculus of who is deserving and who is unworthy of the kindness of strangers in the city.

Moral identities are created at the confluence of how people characterize themselves and what others say about them. If transport workers present themselves as ethical urban actors, some of this self-presentation is corroborated by others. Some young middle-class women recall with gratitude small acts of care from older taxi drivers, such as helping a newcomer in the city to carry heavy luggage and cross a busy thoroughfare. A middle-aged man remembers receiving a call from his young son's phone, to be informed by an autorickshaw driver that the boy's leg had been scrapped in a freak accident and assuring him that the driver would be next to the boy until his father collected the dazed child. Traffic police too are prompt to appreciate the reliability of drivers in situations of crisis. Be it ferrying people in distress who have lost their wallets, taking someone who has been in an accident to the hospital, clearing obstructions from the roads after a stormy day, it is transport workers whom the police depend on to keep people moving in the city. Such expressions of what might be called "handyman masculinity" on the street make cities safe and functional for the urban public. This is a form of moral masculinity that has both the hardiness to execute physically onerous labor and the willingness to do so for the benefit of the urban public. If such acts of goodness from working-class men offer support during city living, they are set against the selfish indifference of the urban middle classes who are said to quickly turn a blind eye to the suffering of strangers. This seems to be the consensus: the taxi operator will alight from his vehicle to help an elderly man suddenly disoriented by a dizzy spell; the person traveling in their automobile will simply drive off.

If, for the most part, traffic police acknowledge the helpful ethic of transport workers, this does not always preclude distrust. A migrant taxi driver recalls encountering a drunken man traveling with a young girl of about eight or nine; something about his demeanor didn't seem right to the driver, and he began questioning

whether the girl was related to him. This frightened the man, and he took off, leaving the girl in the cab. Ironically, when the taxi driver took this girl to the police station and explained the scenario, the officer in charge interrogated him for hours, suspecting the driver of failed abduction. This experience made the driver wary of doing good to strangers on city streets. Middle-class suspicions about the intentions of working-class men in the city

extend to state actors as well, and when law enforcement personnel misconstrue acts of goodness as unlawful conduct, such mis-
characterization weakens the urban poor's intention to do good to
strangers in the city.

Embodiment in the spaces of shared mobility is mediated by
ethical considerations as well. There are drivers and male passengers who deliberately take up more space and are perceived by other
drivers and passengers as inconsiderate—their selfish actions make
the journey uncomfortable for fellow commuters and harm business because the autorickshaw then seems less desirable as a mode
of transit. There are men who physically position themselves in
ways that enable them to grope women co-passengers. And then
there are those—both drivers and passengers—who adopt postures
that clearly signal to women co-travelers in the vehicle that they will
not be harmed. Such styles of bodily comportment in the spaces
of commuting cohere into commuter identities that are the outcome
of moral evaluations of the conduct of strangers.

As drivers see it, there is a moral calculus to intervening in situations where a woman passenger is being sexually harassed by a
co-passenger or fellow driver. Some drivers will reprimand the
perpetrator only when the concerned woman protests, the reasoning being that it is itself immoral to wrongly characterize someone's action as immoral. Hence, they would prefer to wait for
confirmation—in the form of a woman's protests—before acting.
Other drivers observe a different moral economy; they consider it
an ethical necessity to intervene the very moment they notice sexual harm being perpetrated. The moral impulse to do so stems as
much from patriarchal logics of men as protectors of women
and privacy as a prerequisite of sexual contact as from ideas about
bodily autonomy that erotic advances where such interest is unwel-
come are wrong. Transport workers' styles of intervention when
they encounter women being sexual harassed on city streets
create a moral environment that exceeds the limits of the event.
When drivers single out repeat offenders and shame them with
disapproving looks and by refusing to accept their business, this
creates an ambient moral milieu around the circuits of public

transportation that conditionally expands women's access to mobility opportunities in the city. This moral environment in which transport workers are ethical urban actors competes against another milieu in which drivers themselves are singled out for inflicting sexual harm on women passengers. One plank of moral justification used by the middle classes for illtreating transport workers is the former's conviction that drivers misbehave with women and hence are "bad" men.

The body of the vehicle, as a site of men's labor and as a form of public provisioning, is often interpellated through moral terms that proscribe certain forms of behavior in it. For many traffic personnel, nonreligious decorative items, gaudy embellishments, and loud music, besides being unlawful, are morally polluting. When they encounter such items, traffic law enforcement officers will often use the metaphor of a bar—a place of alcohol-fueled depravity in this system of description—to rebuke drivers. For several drivers, passengers making out in the backseat is a defilement of the vehicle because it is an instrument of work. Pleasure, be it sexual, aesthetic, or sensorial, is deemed antithetical to the virtue of work. The sacrality of the public vehicle derives from its provisioning function in the city—a public good—and from it being a source of economic sustenance for drivers and their families—the good family man provides. The public transport vehicle is sacred because it sustains life—the private lives of drivers and the public life of the city.

While the good city is one that is premised on socially progressive values, the safe city affords security within the boundaries of existing social divides. The safe city—as distinct from the good city—can be glimpsed in men's sexual noninvolvement with women commuters. If women experience the male city as one where they must routinely deflect unwanted sexual advances, survive sexual violence, and eke out space for sexual expression, their access to city spaces is enabled when men practice sexual indifference to women in the city. The reasons behind men's sexual indifference to women's presence in the urban outdoors, as we have seen, range from the patriarchal exaltation of monogamy to migrant men identifying the spatial location of their sexual subjectivities in the countryside rather than the city and conceptions of sin being borne by children of parents who have acted wrongfully. Some migrant drivers choose to stay clear of any sexually intimate interactions with women—whether consensual or forced—because of the social consequences of these relations being reported in their villages. The fear of being morally shamed and its far-reaching impact on their families in the village influence migrant drivers' moral choices in the city. Thus, rumors in the village about men's unethical behavior in the city function as a form of social control. Such an ethic of indifference, while not feminist, conditionally abates the threat of gender-based violence on city streets and creates spaces of safety and sexual pleasure for women passengers in the interiors of public vehicles.

An image of the good city, one that is not merely safe but also just, is captured in moments when men enjoy simply seeing acts of heterosexual intimacy in public vehicles as an erotic urban theater without expecting to participate in it. Such forms of voyeurism legitimize quasi-public spaces as a site of heterosexual lust in an urban climate of vigilantism that fixes the sexually active woman as indefensible against rape. The good city emerges in the moral assertions of some male transport workers that women have the right to refuse sexual contact from strangers in public spaces. The good city can also be glimpsed in anecdotes of consensual erotic encounters between drivers and working-class women in the city. These instances distill what a good city might entail because they enable women to experience sexual autonomy in the city on their own terms. However, it is an urban sexual matrix that does not easily allow sexual desire to cross lines of caste and class.

City Characters

At the intersections of everyday morality and the mores of urban commuting, a cast of urban characters can be identified. Although sociologists often relegate the term "character" to the domains of personality psychology and philosophy, there is also a tradition within sociological research that reads characters, especially their moral qualities, as outcomes of social processes and human agency (Sayer 2020). "Character" is the ethical value people place on their desires and their relations to others (Sennett 1998), but it is also the ascription of moral meanings to other people and places. Characters are as much about self-presentation as they are about features attributed to others; and places as much as people can be characters. One can speak, for instance, of the character of a neighborhood or the character of a bookstore; and certainly, cities have characters too. The intensity of a city's charisma may be so great as to seep into the character of people living there (Hansen and Verkaaik 2009). The characterization of people and places as having recognizable attributes and styles of functioning creates a predictable pattern for urban dwellers—if people and places can be expected to behave in certain ways, this reduces the inherent uncertainty of urban life. It is a way of discerning friends and foes in the city, separating the good from the bad. Such everyday practices of moral characterization, as a folk knowledge system about the city, are a measure of both urban survival strategies and urban social inequality. Everyday moral judgments enable people to survive the protean nature of city life; and what moral discourses are enlisted by who and in what context tells us about urban social differences.

Literary scholar Jane Gallop (2002) speaks of "anecdotal theory" as a mode of theorizing that is premised on narrative, stories, and proverbs, toying with words and language. She clarifies that precisely because the "anecdote" and "theory" are seen as polarities—the former being personal, brief, and specific, and the latter being impersonal, broad, and far-reaching—to do "anecdotal theory" is to cut across these oppositions. It is to present theory anecdotally, thereby tying theorizing to storytelling, which is attached to the contextual and the trivial while offering illumination. In anecdotal theory, the example and the generality this example illustrates become indistinguishable and the grandness of theoretical claims simmers down to become occasional. The anecdote conjures associative meanings that exceed the specificity of the event without claiming representativeness. The urban characters that are recognizable in the spaces of commuting emerge through the many anecdotes that urban dwellers tell about their encounters in the city. Like characters in a fictional world, we may understand city characters not through any over-arching definition of types but by "looking at how we talk about them, how we use and respond to them" (Moi 2019, 61), through descriptions and a series of stories that serve as both example and theory.

This is how a story may begin:

THE SPOILED RICH WOMAN

A muggy summer afternoon. Temperatures hovering around forty degrees Celsius. A vacant taxi is trudging along on the empty road; very few have ventured out at this time on such a suffocating day. Enervated by the cruel weather, the taxi driver decides to retire until sundown. He sees a woman, perhaps in her early twenties, waving frantically at him asking him for a ride. She is dressed in expensive, stylish clothes, and for a moment the driver wonders why she is hailing a cab instead of calling her personal chauffeur to take her to her destination in her airconditioned car. As he slows down near her to ask which way she is headed, the taxi driver notices two young children in their teens, looking at him crest-fallen. They had also been waiting for a taxi and look absolutely defeated at the prospect of having to wait indefinitely for the next available cab. When the taxi driver apologetically explains to the young woman that he will ferry the kids and not her because they seem near collapse from the heat, she becomes irate and threaten-ing. Since she had hailed him before the children had, she deserves to be prioritized. She assures the driver that she would use every social influence to ensure that he would pay the heaviest of penal-ties if he took the children and not her.

The following day, the driver is summoned to a police sta-tion. The young woman is present, along with her influential father. The driver is made to recount the events of the previous day. His defenses fall on deaf ears. He is unable to persuade his audience that he was right to prioritize the children. In the face of aggressive questioning by the officer in charge at the police station and a litany of accusations from the woman and her father, the driver finds himself ensnared in logical traps and fails to defend himself. When the driver is finally allowed to leave the station, he has been fined an amount equal to several days' earnings. As he walks to his taxi and drives off, he resolves to never interact with young women of high social class. He associates them with bratty behavior, with powerful fathers, with humiliation. The spoiled upper-class young woman is trouble.

THE SADISTIC POLICEMAN AND THE KIND ONE

There is one type of policeman whom drivers of transport vehicles must watch out for. And that's the sadistic policeman who relishes wielding power over the urban public. This particular traffic sergeant walks with swagger. His gait bears an awareness of the uniform he is wearing and the respect it exacts from others. An autorickshaw driver remembers being stopped by this sergeant and being questioned about the floral decorations in his vehicle. He was still new in the trade, didn't have a full grip on the ropes. And so he spoke back to the sergeant: "Yes, I have some flowers here, so what?" The driver recalls the chilling warning he received from the sergeant in response. With a smile on his face, the sergeant told him, "Remember this forever: every time I stop you on the road, you will lose, and I will win. Remember this for as long as you are an auto driver. And recount this to all your friends. If I stop any of you, it's never for nothing; it means you will part with some. I don't care how you will feed your family. My rules, I don't let anyone get way with ignoring." Stories such as this circulate among drivers, and they know that the best way to deal with the sadistic traffic policeman is to avoid and to defer.

But there is also the kind policeman, such as the one who was called on by an angry male passenger in his late thirties to reprimand a taxi driver for refusing a short-distance trip. Instead of berating the driver, the cop urged the passenger to be more understanding: The driver had managed to find a spot to park his vehicle. If he took the passenger to the mall that was a mere ten-minute walk away, he would have to give up that spot and keep moving after the ride because parking space for taxis is so insufficient in the city. The fare for such a brief trip would not compensate for the fuel costs the driver would incur in remaining on the move. The traffic policeman urged the passenger to understand that without factoring in these calculations, taxi drivers would not be able to sustain their families. The driver recalls stray conversations with this cop. Fleeting exchanges while paying for tea or snacks at a roadside food stall. Brief disclosures of biographical details. A nod of recognition sometimes. That's all.

INCONSIDERATE AND FRIENDLY PASSENGERS

This taxi driver clearly recalls the day he realized that city people care only about themselves. He was very sure that the lane was a one-way street. But the two passengers insisted that they knew the locality well and it was okay to drive down that lane. The driver yielded to their insistence and within minutes was stopped by a traffic policeman. The driver stepped out of the vehicle to plead with the cop to indulge him, to not impose a heavy fine. It was not to be. The taxi driver had to pay. When he returned to his vehicle, he found that the passengers, for whom he had taken the wrong turn, were gone. Seeing trouble with the police, they had simply left without paying the fare. Such passengers don't consider taxi drivers to be humans, people who are brothers, sons, fathers, husbands. For them drivers are no different from machines that get people from point A to point B.

What then makes passengers likeable? "If a passenger treats me like a brother, I will also treat him like one." There is a young chap, a sales executive for an insurance company. He mainly works in the neighborhoods along which this young auto driver operates. He is one of his regular passengers, commuting by his autorickshaw every day of the week, often several times in a day. They speak. Know quite a bit about each other's lives. The insurance guy is working hard to buy an apartment. He wants to move his aging parents out of the damp rental home. He wants to marry a girl he has been seeing. The driver appreciates that he spontaneously shares such details about his life. This is the type of passenger who doesn't maintain a distance of superiority with the driver. Their jobs pay more, they are much more socially respectable than auto driving. But there is also a mutual understanding that they are both basically striving for the same things, trying their best to provide a good life for their kin.

THE LUSTFUL MAN

Such men reveal themselves over time: typically middle-aged, picking autorickshaws depending on who else is sitting inside, waiting for vehicles that have young women passengers, taking up more space than required, gazing lasciviously, and using an array of imagined factors such as inclement weather, paucity of space, and carrying a lot of bags as excuses for unwanted touching.

The type exists among transport workers too. The taxi driver who almost rams his vehicle into the car in front of him, distracted by an attractive woman on the road. The autorickshaw driver who has a special liking for girls from northeast India and who tries his best to get them to sit beside him in the front of the vehicle. Such actions sully the purpose and identity of the vehicle as a public good. What is meant to serve becomes a source of harm. They also provoke a male anxiety about failing to protect women kin from other men's sexual interest. "If these men are feeling up women passengers, surely they don't spare my wife and mother either when they are traveling?"

DANGEROUS PEOPLE, PLACES, AND TIMES

Night is when you need your wits about you the most. But nights tend to dull your alertness. You submit to its influence, and that's when danger strikes. Like the night this taxi driver got mugged. A young woman had hailed him desperately. She had lost her bag with her phone and wallet, she said. Her child had fallen sick. But the child was nowhere to be seen. She explained that she had laid him down on the pavement and had run around the corner to look for a taxi to take them home. Could the driver please come with her and help carry the child? Around the corner a gang of men were waiting for him. They doused him, stole his money, and drove off with his vehicle. The scheming woman posing as a passenger, who uses vulnerability as a ploy to entrap, that's one type of person to avoid in the city.

The other source of danger is the Muslim-majority neighborhood. For the outsider, the Muslim-majority neighborhood is construed as a space of squalor, of criminal activity, of gang-like relations, of violent masculinity. Some encounters become a cautionary tale. Such as the time a taxi driver picked up two Muslim men from one such neighborhood, late in the evening. He was surprised when one sat in front beside him while the other took the usual passenger's seat behind. Within moments of starting the trip, the man sitting next to the driver whipped out a revolver and began patting the driver's thigh with it. "Take the shortest route and be fast. Otherwise, I'll send you on the shortest route to hell." As he drove, petrified, he overheard the two men discussing the contents of the trunk they were carrying—handmade bombs—and how they would store it once they reached their neighborhood. If he survived that trip, the driver resolved to never drive to a Muslim-majority neighborhood at night. For him, such neighborhoods became synonymous with the violent character of the two men he ferried that night.

Studies of the moral worlds of working-class communities show how the working poor disassociate moral value from socioeconomic status to identify other indices—such as self-disciplining, responsible conduct, toil as virtue—to create moral worth (Lamont 2000; Pandian 2008). Recent work on the sociology of morality draws a useful distinction between "thin" and "thick" morality. While thin morality entails relatively easy judgments about what is good and appropriate in a given situation, thick morality involves the creation of moral identities and practices over a longer duration that seep into how social institutions operate (Hitlin and Vaisey 2013). The urban characters that become recognizable in the spaces of commuting capture the workings of a thin morality that, over time and through repeated anecdotal invocation, hardens into a thick morality of the city. The temporality of transit life disallows in-depth knowledge flows between drivers, passengers, and police. Consequently, the city characters that emerge through these interactions are flat, devoid of the rounded details of intimate biographies. The routines of movement make possible a light-touch knowing of strangers; but such surface interpretation is sufficient for the purpose that urban characters are conjured: identify sources of danger and support, conflict and cooperation, appropriate and wrongful conduct, the fickle and the reliable in city living. In the city as a community of strangers, character types are needed to register dependable impressions of people and places that are only somewhat familiar. Such thin morality, through repeated storytelling, invokes relatively stable urban characters and becomes a more encompassing social filter through which copresence in transit spaces becomes discernible.

Men's Morality in the City

How do we speak of gendered subjectivities in the shared spaces of urban mobility? In her essay "Mr. Bennett and Mrs. Brown," Virginia Woolf writes, "Everyone in this room is a judge of character. Indeed, it would be impossible to live for a year without disaster unless one practiced character-reading and had some skill in the art. Our marriages, our friendships depend on it; our business largely depends on it; every day questions arise which can only be solved by its help" (cited in Anderson 2019, 128). In this passage, the identification of character assessment as a skill and its role in averting mishaps and negotiating social relations are instructive for a sociology of the interactive spaces of urban mobilities. The city as a space of flows demands that its inhabitants nurture the ability to maneuver copresence with strangers and avoid contretemps and peril; and doing so successfully entails moral assessments of strangers.

Ethnographies of the social worlds of industrial labor in India reveal that the morality of kinship extends beyond the family to mediate relations between employer and worker in the factory (De Neve 2008). At several moments of encounter on public transport, the private domains of family and intimacy become enmeshed in the public worlds of labor and urban sociability. Interactions between drivers, passengers, and traffic police in commuting spaces are routinely shaped by kin morality. An abiding concern of sociologies of morality has been to understand the moral motivations of social action and uncover the moral schemas that influence social behavior (Hitlin and Vaisey 2013). It is useful to consider, therefore, the moral principles that legitimize investing the public life of cities with familial values. If men understand city life and urban mobility through a moral vocabulary of family relationships, this is to be partially explained by the figure of the "householder" or *grhastha* that has historically embodied a hegemonic masculinity life project in the region.

In the Brahmanical system of thought, the key figure around whom *dharma* (which connotes right living and right being) hinges is the householder, who is endowed with the responsibility of discharging the debts with which every person is born (Heesterman 1981). The householder is the man in the world associated with the virtue of social reproduction and entrusted with the duty of establishing and sustaining the family (Osella and Osella 1999). The crux of the householder's ethic is creating, providing for, protecting, and making sacrifices for his family. As T. N. Madan (2003, 302) writes, in Hindu society the householder "embodies the values of righteousness and action, purity and auspiciousness, and purposefulness and contentment. It is the good life." The moral economy of the family in India exacts the sacrifice of self-interest for the larger good of the family, and this ethic of self-abnegation and duty drives the patriarch or the proverbial head of the family, whose responsibility it is to provide and protect (Uberoi 2006). The domestication of interactions on public transportation is a social effect of the ideological influence of the householder as a moral figure on men's lives. If in men's accounts the social life of public transportation is repeatedly marked by an idiom of kinship, this stems from the moral reasoning that the ideal city is one that facilitates the householder to dislodge his responsibilities toward his family. The interactional order of urban commuting operates in an ethical system in which men's duties within family condition their reflexes to the unknown and the familiar that make up urban living. In this sense, the moral making of a city of men derives substantially from the householder ideology that governs men's lives in the region. But what work does the operation of private morality in public spaces do to everyday life in the city? The playing out of conflict and cooperation on public transport suggests a tacit demand on behalf of men that the public morality in cities that shapes urban citizenship in the substantive sense ought to support the maintenance of sexual division of labor in the family. In other words, the adjudication of conduct in city spaces ought to be premised on the compulsions of the householder ethic, which situates adult men as providers and protectors of their families. The salience of the householder ethic in men's urban lives shows that the gendered morality of family life well exceeds the doorsteps of the home to condition everyday encounters in the city.

Public transport is a social terrain that is peopled by character types with discrete moral temperaments. The frameworks through which such characters get recognized reveal how men navigate the city as moral agents. As a migrant taxi driver put it, "One has to think of good and bad when on the road." Transport workers and commuters thus establish figural patterns in the many encounters they have while moving through the city. While characters are seen as fundamental to reading or viewing any fictional form, this chapter has suggested that characters are salient for how the city is both experienced by residents and understood sociologically. The word "character" refers to persons in a fictional world as well as to the mental and moral traits that distinguish individuals. Recognizing the character types that make up everyday city living highlights the role of ordinary morality in urban social relations. The stories through which urban characters come alive provide a narrative structure to how people make moral sense of copresence in the city.

Urban characters reveal what has been described as "the moral landscape of mobility" (Doherty 2020). Feminists have long pointed out that patriarchal morality constrains women's urban lives in a number of ways. The discussion in this section of the book has sought to highlight what patriarchal morality does to men's lives in the city. The sociology of urban commuting offered in this chapter shows how interactions in the spaces of urban commuting become the locus of moral attention and how such everyday morality participates in the social reproduction of cities for men.

Conclusion

Urbanizing Masculinity Studies

A problem that has proved intractable to feminist readings of urban life is the sheer resilience of patriarchal structures in cities of the postindustrialized world. Notwithstanding vast changes in gender relations, men as a social group continue to exercise enormous power over women in the varied contexts of urban living. In urban India, more middle-class women than ever before are engaged in paid work that requires them to travel outside the home. The present conjuncture is simultaneously a period that is witnessing an unprecedented number of sexual assaults in public spaces being reported in the media. This book has sought to intervene in this conundrum by foregrounding the laboring lives of a mobile group of working-class men in the city of Kolkata.

The crucial insights on gender inequality in cities that feminists have provided coexist with a vast empirical and theoretical gap in understanding the gendered subjectivity of "heterosexual" men's lives in the city. This book represents an effort to attend closely to how men and normative definitions of masculinity infuse the everyday production of the city. At one level, this book has made an empirically grounded presentation of men in quotidian routines of urban mobility. The intention has been to demonstrate how masculine subjectivities in the city are formed in relation to space and movement, and equally how urban spaces and mobilities are structured by masculinities. A key analytical strategy in masculinity studies has been to expose men's claims of universality to be ideological in the sense that they masquerade experiences of men as a general condition. For this reason, feminist scholars have expended effort toward "giving masculinity a history" (Sinha 1999), a narrative that eschews universality in favor of particularity. This book has followed such an analytical cue to give masculinity a distinctly *urban* inflection. It has highlighted how masculinities take up space in the city, and the ways in which urban space constructs masculinities. The project shows that the gendered city and the masculinities of men who inhabit it are coeval.

The pluralizing moment in masculinity studies (Carrigan, Connell, and Lee 1985) has fractured a monolithic understanding of masculinity to recognize not only the multiple ways in which masculinity is performed but also that these versions of masculinity are hierarchically ordered. One pitfall of this otherwise productive conceptual development that refuses a singular notion of masculinity has been that it has produced essentialist views of subcategories such as working-class masculinity, Black masculinity, gay masculinity, and so on (Flood 2002). One way of avoiding such essentialist traps is to use a comparative optic in social research on men and masculinities. Comparison of the different trajectories that similar social phenomena can take can potentially curtail the tendency to make essentialist claims about both people and spaces. This study has implicitly been guided by an intraurban comparative frame, one that uses the idea of "cities within cities" (McFarlane, Silver, and Truelove 2017) to portray the multiple urban worlds that different groups of men move through within a city. By looking at working-class men's varied experiences of Kolkata, the present project conveys the plural meanings that different urban spaces accrue in relation to shifting registers of masculinity. Thus, while most working-class men report a sense of being disrespected and vulnerability to the protean nature of cities, these indignities and deprivations are experienced and managed variously, depending on men's embedment in other social bases such as linguistic community, religion, and spatial location. Men who see themselves as local may take recourse to neighborhood networks they are inserted in to grapple with urban uncertainty, while migrant men may lay claim on cultural discourses of masculinity that bespeak their preparedness to deal with risk.

Ethnographic approaches to men's lives in the city bear testimony to the ideological associations between masculinity and the outdoors; on the other hand, they convey the extent to which the home exceeds the limits of the doorstep to infiltrate the street. If men find pleasure in the city, fear it, discover friendships in urban encounters, ward off hostilities, and seek to escape it or dwell in it with a modicum of permanence, these disparate urban intimations are firmly tied to their place in the heteronormative family. The salience of the private in the public lives of men underlines the need for urban researchers to renew analytical focus on the public/private distinction in the ordering of metropolitan life. By highlighting these connections, the book shows the value that insights from masculinity studies have for understanding urban processes.

The city, as urban scholars have long pointed out, is simultaneously a space of exclusion and inclusion, offering liberatory opportunities as well as accosting urbanites with precarity and danger. In following the everyday movements of male public transport workers in Kolkata, I have identified a few ways in which urban researchers might use the lens of "masculinities" to make sense of how the gendering of city spaces relates to urban uncertainty. I have argued that recognizing the dual pulls of the city, the manner in which urban structures manufacture hazard even as they provide succor, is crucial for understanding the hardiness of patriarchal urban formations. To the extent that critical urban theory has prioritized social inequalities in cities, it has been preoccupied with how urban inequalities are generated and resisted through conflict between different social groups. An influential thread in this literature, however, has been concerned with everyday cooperation and the makeshift forms of urbanism through which urban actors make the city work for them (Simone 2004). The very fact that urban life is thoroughly unequal means that disenfranchised urban publics have to find creative solutions to the problem of survival in the city, an entrepreneurial spirit that in the Indian context is captured in the Hindi word *jugaad*.

Drawing inspiration from this approach in urban studies, the chapters that compose this book have argued that the city is normatively manufactured as a male space through both conflict and cooperation. Indeed, working-class men's labors in the city convey an urban narrative that braids discord with collaboration. To understand the character of friction and collaboration between men in public spaces, I have used the concepts of risk, trust, and homosociality. I have shown that risk in the course of everyday city living is experienced by men primarily as a threat to their role as providers for their families. The cultural impetus to be breadwinners puts men at risk in the sense that social structures of the city variously inhibit and provide avenues for the attainment of this goal. Inhabiting the city as a man means learning how to navigate these constraints and opportunities to one's advantage. These lessons entail identifying, if tenuously, oppositions as well as allies. Even as men position other men as competitors in the urban labor market, they also recognize the similarity between their social motivations. The recognition of the social expectation from men to be providers, as I have shown, may overwrite social differences between men as they encounter each other in the city.

Throughout this discussion, the complex moral provocations of masculinity and how they relate to the making of everyday urban life have been highlighted. In the many stories that transport workers narrate about their mobilities in the city, a crew of urban characters are recognizable and convey the moral terrain of urban life. These characters have distinct moral dispositions and personify the gendered morality through which mobilities are experienced. Men's mutual regard for their provider role, its importance in the survival of their families and their own social worth, creates a culture of morality on city streets that is premised on homosociality. By fashioning such an interactional order, men produce a moral vocabulary and practices through which they tentatively transact trust with strangers and identify threats in the city. This homosocial bond allows men who are otherwise framed in conflicting social relations (such as law enforcement officers and transport workers, "locals" and "outsiders") to find a common ground on which to cope with the vagaries of urban life. The production of such a homosocial culture of trust, as the preceding chapters have demonstrated, has far-reaching consequences for the gendered making of the everyday city. It pervades interactions between drivers, and between drivers and commuters, as well as the legal regulation of mobilities in the city. A male homosocial street culture that sustains the normative connection between masculinity and wage labor simultaneously gives life to an interpretative framework that reads women's presence in the outdoors as an anomaly. In terms of this discourse, women in the city—as temptresses or as claimants on the urban labor market—are seen as detracting from male breadwinning. Thus, if the image of women in public spaces persistently evokes anxiety and rage in Indian cities, these reactions are to be partially explained by a homosocial culture of the street in the region that invests enormous moral value in men's provider role, a powerful index of masculinity that is itself tied to the city.

This book's emphasis on social collaboration in the quotidian city, therefore, far from divesting urban analysis of a focus on gendered power, calls attention to the everyday gestures of support through which the male character of the city is emboldened. Instead of conceptualizing ethnography only as a methodological and interpretive practice that allows the researcher to recuperate hidden social patterns and prod research subjects to divulge what they wish to withhold, I have used ethnography—as a method and as a form of expression—to draw attention to the surfaces of mundane urban encounters. Instead of prying people/situations apart to get at the depths of social meanings, "surface reading" (Best and Marcus 2009) urges the ethnographer to take seriously what is presenting itself to be looked at and not necessarily shielding meanings that lie below it. Such a strategic suspension of the "hermeneutics of suspicion" that characterizes critical theory (Felski 2015) does not eschew focus on social inequality as much as it opens another perspective on it—how everyday forms of cooperation and moral judgments between urban actors are fundamental for upholding structures of power in cities.

To the extent that gender is a relational term, some readers may be concerned by the absence of an explicit discussion of femininity in my project. It seems necessary to clarify, therefore, that while gender is certainly a relational concept, masculinity is relational not simply with respect to femininity but also with respect to other forms of masculinity. Indeed, one of the key theoretical contributions of a sociology of masculinity has been precisely to show the hierarchical ties that structure different formations of maleness. Relationality exists both within and among genders. In this study, the relational aspect of gender has been brought out by throwing light on the multiple spatial trajectories that different masculinities follow, rather than by an overt consideration of masculinity in relation to femininity. Nevertheless, precisely because men's public lives are so profoundly impacted by their relations with women in the private domain—and this is a key analytical point that I have made throughout the preceding chapters—femininity appears in my book as a residual category. To make sense of men's public careers in the city I have considered at length their private roles, especially in relation to women in their families.

This book began with two questions: How do men inhabit the city? How do these modes of being produce the city as a gendered space? In responding to these concerns, it now seems necessary to address a third question: What does an emphasis on the urban contribute to the study of men and masculinities? The remainder of this concluding chapter tackles this question and, in doing so, makes a plea for urbanizing masculinity studies.

A critique that is often leveled at masculinity studies is that after an initial burst of robust theoretical innovation, it has settled into simply finding new contexts in which to relay a familiar narrative of the social construction of masculinities. This is one reason why the field has remained a narrow, specialist terrain. Thinking about the future of masculinity studies, several scholars (Connell 2003) have suggested that it ought to go beyond an individualist approach to examine the masculinist character of large-scale institutions such as the state, corporations, international relations, trade, and global markets; such an emphasis on global processes and institutions requires the adoption of a transnational lens (Hearn 2019). Living, as we do, in an interconnected world, it is vital to think about the gender order at the scale of the globe. In this vision of the future of masculinity studies, the "urban" is noticeably absent. There is by now a considerable body of geographical scholarship on masculinities in which the question of place and space has been fundamental; but the specificity of urbanization as a sociospatial process remains to be examined in a sustained way by scholars of masculinities. This is striking because urbanization is a planetary phenomenon to the extent that the human condition and the urban condition might well have become synonymous (Amin 2013). The invitation to do masculinity studies in a global perspective and urban scholars' argument that urbanization has a global reach share considerable conceptual ground. Indeed, if cities are experimenting with the art of being global (Roy and Ong 2011), such urban renovations parallel the need identified by scholars of gender for "worlding" masculinity studies as a terrain of feminist inquiry. These conceptual synergies between urban studies and the critical study of men and masculinities ought to be brought into sustained dialogue. Since so much of men's everyday lives is impacted by the global scale of urbanization processes, scholarly efforts to arrive at a deeper understanding of the contemporary meanings of masculinity would do well to incorporate perspective from urban studies. Ignoring the urban while attempting to theorize the workings of a world gender order scants masculinity studies of a valuable intellectual tradition with which it can usefully consort.

There are some compelling reasons why unraveling the masculinities of the global gender order would benefit from attending to urbanization. The global macro-processes that have been identified as vital to study through the lens of masculinities, if we are to widen the intellectual scope of this research field, are acutely observable in city spaces. Cities—especially global cities—are a spatial moment in which globalization processes are visible in a particularly pronounced form (Sassen 2000). The centralization of control operations of financial firms entails creating offshore affiliates—factories and serviced outlets—outside of their home countries. Here, cities emerge as key nodes because they house these functions of global corporations (Sassen 2000). In doing so, cities capture the complex transnational and translocal dynamics of globalization processes that manufacture both new hegemonic and subversive gender projects. The power of global cities resides in their function as hubs of knowledge and innovation, as well as the political, cultural, and infrastructural assets they harbor (Amin 2013). If the future of masculinity studies resides in studying power structures on a global scale (Connell 2016), the importance of urbanization processes in the production of the global economy and, hence, the world gender order needs to be confronted by scholars of masculinities as a mode of investigating gendered power on a global scale.

None of this is to suggest that masculinity studies becomes a mere subset of urban studies. Indeed, it has been important to acknowledge and address the inadequate attention paid to men's lives in nonurban, especially rural, contexts (Campbell and Bell 2000). It is not to insist on "methodological cityism," which has been critiqued for focusing all urban investigation on the city to the exclusion of wider urbanization processes (Angelo and Wachshmuth 2015). Rather, it is to suggest that even those studies that aim to understand nonmetropolitan forms of masculinity would profit from engaging with the expansive reach of urbanization processes in the contemporary world. Even as cities hold a mirror to macro processes that operate at a global scale, urbanization is no longer restricted to the form of human settlement commonly identified as cities. Rather, the planetary scale of urbanization has produced what is being called "landscapes of extended urbanization," which cannot be thought of as "rural" but are an intrinsic part of the logics of urbanization (Brenner and Schmid 2015). Urban questions have moved to the center of public and academic debates on the major social problems assailing societies today and are hence integral to identifying solutions to them. This has been happening at a time when there are large-scale spatial transformations that are underway: (1) city regions are expanding into larger urban agglomerations in ways that explode the urban/rural divide; (2) the urban is seen as the primary site for contentious politics, such that changing the conditions of urban life is seen as fundamental to transforming broader political-economic arrangements (Brenner 2013). The influence of the urban is thus felt also in traditionally nonurban locations such as the village and the countryside, in the forms of workers who commute to the city, media, and urbanized lifestyles (Amin and Thrift 2017). Historically, it is by recognizing that gendered power has global dimensions that research on masculinity gained importance as a key explanatory factor in the making of globalization (Connell 2012). It is precisely because urbanization has become the principal modality of provisioning for life, in its broadest sense, that the urbanization of masculinity studies will once again enable this terrain of inquiry to resist being ghettoized as a specialist field.

In an urban age, "knowing the world might require knowing the city" (Amin and Thrift 2017, 10). Thus, while the birth of urban studies might be traced to a moment when the "city" was separated out from "society" as a distinct object of inquiry, that moment seems to have passed as the division between urban and society becomes increasingly difficult to sustain in the present day. How might masculinity studies open itself up to urbanization processes at local and planetary scales? How might we understand urbanisms through the lens of masculinities? This book has made one such possible intervention by spurring thought to the quarrels as well as fellowship between different formations of masculinity through which a city of men comes into being.

Acknowledgments

At various stages of preparation, several people read and commented on different sections of this book and offered valuable words of encouragement. For their generosity and support which enabled me to complete this project, I am very grateful to Sanjay Srivastava, Abdoumaliq Simone, Chua Beng Huat, Jan Willem Duyvendak, Ranjana Raghunathan, Gaurav Mittal, Ambika Aiyadurai, Sagnik Dutta, Zaid Al Baset, Suzi Hall, Eric C. Thompson, Raka Ray, Peter van der Veer, Pedram Dibazar, Colin McFarlane, Tina Harris, Rivke Jaffe, Fran Martin, Tapati Guha-Thakurta, Niko Besnier, Hung-Ying Chen, Diego García-Mejuto, Sol Gamsu, Sibaji Bandyopadhyay, Marguerite van den Berg, Supratik Barik, Pranab Basu, Sylvia Chant, Jane M. Jacobs, Tora Holmberg, Christian Schmid, and Łukasz Froncek.

The support of my colleagues at Erasmus University College in Rotterdam has been of great help. Sincerest thanks especially to Roy Kemmers, Ward Vloeberghs, Gera Noordzij, and Alexander Strelkov.

Fieldwork for this book was funded by a grant from the Faculty of Arts and Social Sciences, National University of Singapore.

Cover art and interior book illustrations were created by Subhajit Das.

Sections of chapter 2 appeared as an article: "The Social Life of Transport Infrastructures: Masculinities and Everyday Mobilities in Kolkata" in *Urban Studies* 58(1), 73–89. https://doi.org/10.1177/0042098019875420. Sections of chapter 4 were published as an article entitled "Homosocial Trust in Urban Policing: Masculinities and Traffic Law Enforcement in the Gendered City" in *CITY: Analysis of Urban Change, Theory, Action* 24:3–4, 493–511. DOI: 10.1080/13604813.2020.1781410.

At Rutgers University Press, Kim Guinta saw value in this project and shepherded it to completion.

And finally, my deepest thanks to the people who are at the center of this book: the autorickshaw and taxi operators, the traffic police personnel, and the commuters who shared with me stories of their lives in the city.

References

Adeel, M., A. Gar-On Yeh, and F. Zhang. 2016. "Transportation Disadvantage and Activity Participation in the Cities of Rawalpindi and Islamabad, Pakistan." *Transport Policy* 47: 1–12.

Agrawal, A., ed. 2006. *Migrant Women and Work*. New Delhi: Sage.

Agrawal, A., and A. Sharma. 2015. "Gender Contests in the Delhi Metro: Implications of Reservation of a Coach for Women." *Indian Journal of Gender Studies* 22 (3), 421–436.

Ahmad, Z., Z. Batool, and P. Starkey. 2019. "Understanding Mobility Characteristics and Needs of Older Persons in Urban Pakistan with Respect to Use of Public Transport and Self-driving." *Journal of Transport Geography* 74: 181–190.

Amin, A. 2012. *Land of Strangers*. Cambridge: Polity.

———. 2013. "The Urban Condition: A Challenge to Social Science." *Public Culture* 25 (2): 201–208.

———. 2014. "Lively Infrastructure." *Theory, Culture & Society* 31 (7/8): 137–161.

Amin, A., and N. Thrift. 2002. *Cities: Reimagining the Urban*. Cambridge: Polity.

———. 2017. *Seeing Like a City*. Cambridge: Polity.

Amrute, S. 2015. "Moving Rape: Trafficking in the Violence of Postliberalization." *Public Culture* 17 (2): 331–359.

Anderson, A. 2019. "Thinking with Character." In *Character: Three Inquiries in Literary Studies*, edited by A. Anderson, R. Felski, and T. Moi, 127–170. Chicago: University of Chicago Press.

Anderson, E. 1990. *Streetwise: Race, Class, and Change in an Urban Community*. Chicago: University of Chicago Press.

Anderson, E., and M. McCormack. 2016. "Inclusive Masculinity Theory: Overview, Reflection and Refinement." *Journal of Gender Studies* 27 (5): 547–561.

Angelo, H., and C. Hentschel. 2015. "Interactions with Infrastructure as Windows into Social Worlds: A Method for Critical Urban Studies." *City* 19 (2–3): 306–312.

Angelo, H., and D. Wachsmuth. 2015. "Urbanizing Urban Political Ecology: A Critique of Methodological Cityism." *International Journal of Urban and Regional Research* 39 (1): 16–27.

Anjaria, J. S. 2011. "Ordinary States: Everyday Corruption and the Politics of Space in Mumbai." *American Ethnologist* 38 (1): 58–72.

Anjaria, J. S., and C. McFarlane, eds. 2011. *Urban Navigations: Politics, Space and the City in South Asia*. New Delhi: Routledge.

Annavarapu, S. 2022. "Risky Routes, Safe Suspicions: Gender, Class, and Cabs in Hyderabad, India." *Social Problems* 69 (3): 761–780.

Appadurai, A. 2004. "The Capacity to Aspire: Culture and the Terms of Recognition." In *Culture and Public Action*, edited by V. Rao and M. Walton, 59–84. Stanford, CA: Stanford University Press.

Asad, T. 2004. "Where Are the Margins of the State?" In *Anthropology in the Margins of the State*, edited by V. Das and D. Poole, 279–288. Santa Fe, NM: School of American Research Press.

Auyero, J., and K. Sobering. 2019. *The Ambivalent State: Police–Criminal Collusion at the Urban Margin*. Oxford: Oxford University Press.

Bagchi, J. 1990. "Women since Independence." In *Calcutta: The Living City*, vol. 2, edited by S. Chaudhuri, 42–49. Calcutta: Oxford University Press.

Balachandran, C. S. 2004. "A Preliminary Report on Emerging Gay Geographies in Bangalore, India." In *Sexual Sites, Seminal Attitudes: Sexualities, Masculinities and Culture in South Asia*, edited by S. Srivastava, 165–187. New Delhi: Sage.

Balkmar, D. 2014. "Negotiating the 'Plastic Rocket': Masculinity, Car Styling and Performance in the Swedish Modified Car Community." *NORMA: International Journal for Masculinity Studies* 9 (3): 166–177.

Banerjee, H. 2012. "The Other Sikhs: Punjabi-Sikhs of Kolkata." *Studies in History* 28 (2): 271–300.

Bates, L., E. Antrobus, S. Bennett, and P. Martin. 2015. "Comparing Police and Public Perceptions of a Routine Traffic Encounter." *Police Quarterly* 18: 442–468.

Baviskar, A. 2002. "The Politics of the City." *Seminar* 516 (August): 40–42.

Bayley, D. H. 1969. *Police and Political Development in India.* Princeton, NJ: Princeton University Press.

Beasley, C. 2005. *Gender and Sexuality: Critical Theories, Critical Thinkers.* London: Sage.

Bech, H. 1998. "Citysex: Representing Lust in Public." *Theory, Culture and Society* 15 (3–4): 215–241.

Bengry-Howell, A. 2005. "Performative Motorcar Display: The Cultural Construction of Young Working Class Masculine Identities." PhD dissertation, University of Birmingham.

Benjamin, W. 2006. *Berlin Childhood Around 1900.* Translated by Howard Eiland. Cambridge, MA: Harvard University Press.

Berg, L. D., and R. Longhurst. 2003. "Placing Masculinities and Geography." *Gender, Place & Culture* 10 (4): 351–360.

Best, S., and S. Marcus. 2009. "Surface Reading: An Introduction." *Representations* 108 (1): 1–21.

Bird, S. R. 1996. "Welcome to the Men's Club: Homosociality and the Maintenance of Hegemonic Masculinity." *Gender & Society* 10 (2): 120–132.

Bissell, D. 2010. "Passenger Mobilities: Affective Atmospheres and the Sociality of Public Transport." *Environment and Planning D: Society and Space* 28 (2): 270–289.

Bittner, E. 1967. "The Police on Skid-Row: A Study of Peace Keeping." *American Sociological Review* 32 (5): 699–715.

Blokland, T. 2017. *Community as Urban Practice.* Cambridge: Polity.

Bondi, L., and D. Rose. 2003. "Constructing Gender, Constructing the Urban: A Review of Anglo-American Feminist Urban Geography." *Gender, Place & Culture* 10 (3): 229–245.

Bose, P. S. 2015. *Urban Development in India: Global Indians in the Remaking of Kolkata.* London: Routledge.

Boyce, P. 2008. "(Dis)Locating Male-to-Male Sexualities in Calcutta: Subject, Space and Perception." In *The Phobic and the Erotic: The Politics* of *Sexualities in Contemporary India*, edited by B. Bose and S. Bhattacharyya, 399–416. Kolkata: Seagull.

———. 2013. "The Object of Attention: Same-Sex Sexualities in Small-Town India and the Contemporary Sexual Subject." In *Sexuality Studies*, edited by S. Srivastava, 184–214. New Delhi: Oxford University Press.

Brenner, N. 2013. "Theses on Urbanization." *Public Culture* 25 (1): 86–114.

Brenner, N., and C. Schmid. 2015. "Towards a New Epistemology of the Urban." *CITY* 19 (2–3): 151–182.

Brosius, C. 2013. "Love Attacks: Romance, Media Voyeurism and Activism in the Public Domain." In *Sexuality Studies*, edited by S. Srivastava, 255–286. New Delhi: Oxford University Press.

Butler, J. 1997. *The Psychic Life of Power: Theories in Subjection.* Stanford, CA: Stanford University Press.

Campbell, H., and M. M. Bell. 2000. "The Question of Rural Masculinities." *Rural Sociology* 65: 532–546.

Carrigan, T., R. W. Connell, and J. Lee. 1985. "Towards a New Sociology of Masculinity." *Theory and Society* 14 (5): 551–604.

Chakravorty, S. 2000. "From Colonial City to Globalizing City? The Far-From-Complete Spatial Transformation of Calcutta." In *Globalising Cities: A New Spatial Order?*, edited by P. Marcuse and R. van Kempen, 56–77. Oxford: Blackwell.

Charsley, K., and H. Wray. 2015. "Introduction: The Invisible (Migrant) Man." *Men and Masculinities* 18 (4): 403–423.

Chatterjee, A. 2015. "Narratives of Exclusion: Space, Insecurity and Identity in a Muslim Neighbourhood in Kolkata." *Economic and Political Weekly* 52: 92–99.

———. 2017. *Margins of Citizenship: Muslim Experiences in Urban India.* London: Routledge.

Chatterjee, B. 1973. *A Study in the Police Administration in West Bengal.* Kolkata: Apurba.

Chaudhuri, S. 1990. "Traffic and Transport in Calcutta." In *Calcutta: The Living City*, vol. 2: *The Present and Future*, edited by S. Chaudhuri, 148–159. Calcutta: Oxford University Press.

Chopra, R. 2003. "Rethinking Pro-feminism: Men, Work and Family in India." Brasília: United Nations Division for the Advancement of Women.

Chopra, R., C. Osella, and F. Osella, eds. 2004. *South Asian Masculinities: Contexts of Change, Sites of Continuity.* New Delhi: Women Unlimited.

Christensen, M. J. 2004. "Calcutta." In *Encyclopedia of Homelessness*, vol. 1, edited by D. Levinson, 39–41. London: Sage.

Clarsen, G. W. 2013. "Feminism and Gender." In *The Routledge Handbook of Mobilities*, edited by P. Adey, D. Bissell, K. Hannam, P. Merriman, and M. Sheller, 94–102. London: Routledge.

Cohen, P. 1979. "Policing the Working-Class City." In *Capitalism and the Rule of Law*, edited by B. Fine et al., 118–136. London: Hutchinson.

Connell, R. 1990. "The State, Gender, and Sexual Politics: Theory and Appraisal." *Theory and Society* 19: 507–544.

———. 1995. *Masculinities.* Cambridge: Polity.

———. 2003. "Masculinities, Change, and Conflict in Global Society: Thinking about the Future of Men's Studies." *Journal of Men's Studies* 11: 249–266.

———. 2012. Masculinity Research and Global Change. *Masculinities and Social Change* 1 (1): 4–18.

———. 2016. "Masculinities in Global Perspective: Hegemony, Contestation, and Changing Structures of Power." *Theory and Society* 45 (4): 303–318.

Connell, R. W. 1987. *Gender and Power: Society, the Person and Sexual Politics.* Cambridge: Polity.

———. 1996. "New Directions in Gender Theory, Masculinity Research, and Gender Politics." *Ethnos* 61(3–): 157–76.

Connell, R. W., and J. Messerschmidt. 2005. "Hegemonic Masculinity: Rethinking the Concept." *Gender & Society* 16 (9): 829–859.

Cornwall, A., F. G. Karioris, and N. Lindisfarne, eds. 2016. *Masculinities under Neoliberalism.* London: Zed Books.

Corsianos, M. 2009. *Policing and Gendered Justice: Examining the Possibilities.* Toronto: University of Toronto Press.

Dant, T. 2014. "Drivers and Passengers." In *Routledge Handbook of Mobilities*, edited by P. Adey, D. Bissell, K. Hannam, P. Merriman, and M. Sheller, 367–375. London: Routledge.

Das, V. 2004. "The Signature of the State: The Paradox of Illegibility." In *Anthropology in the Margins of the State*, edited by V. Das and D. Poole, 225–254. Santa Fe, NM: School of American Research Press.

Das, V., and D. Poole, eds. 2004. *Anthropology in the Margins of the State*. Santa Fe, NM: School of American Research Press.Datta, A. 2012. *The Illegal City: Space, Law and Gender in a Delhi Squatter Settlement*. Farnham: Ashgate.

Datta, A., and S. K. Mishra. 2011. "Glimpses of Women's Lives in Rural Bihar: Impact of Male Migration." *The Indian Journal of Labour Economics* 54 (3): 457–477.

Day, K., C. Stump, and D. Carreon. 2003. "Confrontation and Loss of Control: Masculinity and Men's Fear in Public Space. *Journal of Environmental Psychology* 23(3), 311–322.

de Haan, A. 2002. "Migration and Livelihoods in Historical Perspective: A Case Study of Bihar, India." *Journal of Development Studies* 38 (5):115–142.

———. 2007. "Diversity in Patterns of Urbanisation: The Long-duree of an Industrial Area in Calcutta." In *Indian Cities in Transition*, edited by A. Shaw, 390–411. Hyderabad: Orient Longman.

DeKeseredy, W. S., and M. D. Schwartz. 2005. "Masculinities and Interpersonal Violence." In *Handbook of Studies on Men and Masculinities*, edited by M. S. Kimmel, J. Hearn, and R. Connell, 353–366. Thousand Oaks, CA: Sage.

Desai, M., ed. 2007. *Gender and the Built Environment in India*. New Delhi: Zubaan.

Dey, I., R. Samaddar, and S. Sen. 2013. *Beyond Kolkata: Rajarhat and the Dystopia of Urban Imagination*. London: Routledge.

Dhillon, M., and S. Bakaya. 2014. "Street Harassment: A Qualitative Study of the Experiences of Young Women in Delhi." *SAGE Open* 4 (3). https://doi.org/10.1177/2158244014543786.

Doherty, J. 2020. "Motorcycle Taxis, Personhood, and the Moral Landscape of Mobility." *Geoforum* 136: 242–250. https://doi.org/10.1016/j.geoforum.2020.04.003.

Donaldson, M., R. Hibbins, R. Howson, and B. Pease, eds. 2009. *Migrant Men: Critical Studies of Masculinities and the Migration Experience*. London: Routledge.

Donaldson, M., and R. Howson. 2009. "Men, Migration and Hegemonic Masculinity." In *Migrant Men: Critical Studies of Masculinities and the*

Migration Experience, edited by M. Donaldson, R. Hibbins, R. Howson, and B. Pease, 210–217. London: Routledge.

Donner, H. 2012. "Whose City Is It Anyway: Middle-Class Imagination and Urban Restructuring in Twenty-First Century Kolkata." *New Perspectives on Turkey* 46: 129–155.

Dutta, N. 2015. "Auto-rickshaw: *Jukti Totthyo Motamot.*" SWS-RLS Occasional Paper 8, School of Women's Studies, Jadavpur University.

Elski, B. 2018. "Police and Masculinities in Transition in Turkey: From Macho to Reformed to Militarized Policing." *Men and Masculinities* 1 (2): 1–25.

Fassin, D. 2013. *Enforcing Order: An Ethnography of Urban Policing.* Cambridge: Polity.

Felski, R. 2015. *The Limits of Critique.* Chicago: University of Chicago Press.

Ferguson, J., and A. Gupta. 2002. "Spatializing States: Toward an Ethnography of Neoliberal Governmentality." *American Ethnologist* 29 (4): 981–1002.

Fernandes, L. 2004. "The Politics of Forgetting: Class Politics and the Restructuring of Urban Space in India." *Urban Studies* 41 (12): 2415–2430.

———. 2006. *India's New Middle Class: Democratic Politics in an Era of Economic Reform.* Minneapolis: University of Minnesota Press.

Flood, M. 2002. "Between Men and Masculinity: An Assessment of the Term 'Masculinity' in Recent Scholarship on Men." In *Manning the Next Millennium: Studies in Masculinities*, edited by S. Pearce and V. Muller, 203–213. Perth: Black Swan.

———. 2008. "Men, Sex, and Homosociality: How Bonds between Men Shape Their Sexual Relations with Women." *Men and Masculinities* 20 (3): 339–359.

Fuller, C., and J. Harris. 2001. "For an Anthropology of the Modern Indian State." In *The Everyday State and Society in Modern India*, edited by C. J. Fuller and V. Bene, 1–30. London: Hurst & Company.

Fyfe, N. R. 1995. "Policing the City." *Urban Studies* 32: 759–778.

Gallop, J. 2002. *Anecdotal Theory.* Durham, NC: Duke University Press.

Ganguly-Scrase, R. 2003. "Paradoxes of Globalization, Liberalization, and Gender Equality: The Worldviews of the Lower Middle Class in West Bengal, India." *Gender and Society* 17 (4): 544–566.

Garcia, C. M., M. E. Eisenberg, E. A. Frerich, K. E. Lechner, and K. Lust. 2012. "Conducting Go-Along Interviews to Understand Context and Promote Health." *Qualitative Health Research* 22 (10): 1395–1403.

Gayer, L., and C. Jaffrelot. 2012. *Muslims in Indian Cities: Trajectories of Marginalisation.* London: Hurst.

Ghertner, D. A. 2015. *Rule by Aesthetics: World-Class City Making in Delhi.* New York: Oxford University Press.

Goel, R. 2018. "Modelling of Road Traffic Fatalities in India." *Accident Analysis and Prevention* 112: 105–115.

Gooptu, N. 2007. "Economic Liberalisation, Work and Democracy: Industrial Decline and Urban Politics in Kolkata." *Economic and Political Weekly* 42 (21): 1922–1933.

———. 2009. "Neoliberal Subjectivity, Enterprise Culture and New Workplaces: Organised Retail and Shopping Malls in India." *Economic and Political Weekly* 44 (22): 45–54.

———. 2013a. "Servile Sentinels of the City: Private Security Guards, Organized Informality and Labour in Interactive Services in Globalized India." *International Review of Social History* 58 (1): 9–38.

———. 2013b. *Enterprise Culture in Neoliberal India: Studies in Youth, Class, Work, and Media.* London: Routledge.

Gopakumar, G. 2015. "Who Will Decongest Bengaluru? Politics, Infrastructures, & Scapes." *Mobilities* 10 (2): 310–325.

Graham, S., ed. 2010. *Disrupted Cities: When Infrastructure Fails.* New York: Routledge.

Graham, S., and S. Marvin. 2001. *Splintering Urbanism: Networked Infrastructures, Technological Mobilities and the Urban Condition.* London: Routledge.

Graham, S., and C. McFarlane, eds. 2014. *Infrastructural Lives. Urban Infrastructure in Context.* New York: Routledge.

Gupta, A. 1995. "Blurred Boundaries: The Discourse of Corruption, the Culture of Politics, and the Imagined State." *American Ethnologist* 22 (2): 375–402.

Gupta, H. 2016. "Taking Action: The Desiring Subjects of Neoliberal Feminism in India." *Journal of International Women's Studies* 17 (1): 152–168.

Gutmann, M. C. 1997. "Trafficking in Men: The Anthropology of Masculinity." *Annual Review of Anthropology* 26: 385–409.

Hammarén, N., and T. Johansson. 2014. "Homosociality: In between Power and Intimacy." *SAGE Open* 4 (1). https://doi.org/10.1177/2158244013518057.

Hammarén, N., and T. Johansson. 2020. "The Transformation of Homosociality." In *Routledge International Handbook of Masculinity Studies*, edited by L. Gottzén, U. Mellström, and T. Shefer, 213–222. London: Routledge.

Hammersley, M., and P. Atkinson. 1995. *Ethnography: Principles in Practice*. London: Routledge.

Hansen, A. 2015. "Transport in Transition: Doi Moi and the Consumption of Cars and Motorbikes in Hanoi." *Journal of Consumer Culture* 17 (2). https://doi.org/10.1177/1469540515602301.

Hansen, A., Nielsen, K. B., eds., 2017. *Cars, Automobility and Development in Asia: Wheels of Change*. Routledge: London.

Hansen, T. B. 1999. *The Saffron Wave: Democracy and Hindu Nationalism in Modern India*. Princeton, NJ: Princeton University Press.

———. 2001a. "Governance and Myths of State in Mumbai." In *The Everyday State and Society in Modern India*, edited by C. J. Fuller and V. Bénéï, 31–67. London: Hurst.

———. 2001b. *Wages of Violence: Naming and Identity in Postcolonial Bombay*. Princeton, NJ: Princeton University Press.

Hansen, T. B., and O. Verkaik. 2009. "Introduction—Urban Charisma on Everyday Mythologies in the City." *Critique of Anthropology* 29 (1): 5–26

Hanson, S., ed. 1995. *The Geography of Urban Transportation*. New York: Guilford.

Hanson, S., and G. Pratt. 1995. *Gender, Work and Space*. London: Routledge.

Hearn, J. 1998. "Theorizing Men and Men's Theorizing: Men's Discursive Practices in Theorizing Men." *Theory and Society* 27 (6): 781–816.

———. 2004. "From Hegemonic Masculinity to the Hegemony of Men." *Feminist Theory* 5: 49–72.

———. 2019. "So What Has Been, Is, and Might Be Going on in Studying Men and Masculinities? Some Continuities and Discontinuities." *Men and Masculinities* 22 (1): 53–63.

Heesterman, J. C. 1981. "Householder and Wanderer." *Contributions to Indian Sociology* 15 (1–2): 251–271.

Hibbins, R., and B. Pease. 2009. "Men and Masculinities on the Move." In *Migrant Men: Critical Studies of Masculinities and the Migration Experience*, edited by M. Donaldson, R. Hibbins, R. Howson, and B. Pease, 1–19. New York: Routledge.

Highmore, B. 2001. "Obligation to the Ordinary: Michel de Certeau, Ethnography and Ethics." *Strategies* 14 (2): 253–263.

Hitlin, S., and Vaisey, S. 2013. "The New Sociology of Morality." *Annual Review of Sociology* 39: 51–68.

Hoelscher, K. 2016. "The Evolution of the Smart Cities Agenda in India." *International Area Studies Review* 19 (1): 28–44.

Holston, J., and A. Appadurai. 1999. "Introduction: Cities and Citizenship." In *Cities and Citizenship*, edited by J. Holston, 1–18. Durham, NC: Duke University Press.

Howson, R. 2009. "Deconstructing Hegemonic Masculinity: Contradiction, Hegemony and Dislocation." *Nordic Journal for Masculinity Studies* 4 (1): 7–21.

Hubbard, P. 2008. "Here, There, Everywhere: The Ubiquitous Geographies of Heteronormativity." *Geography Compass* 2 (3): 640–658.

Hubbard, P., and D. Lyon. 2018. "Introduction: Streetlife—The Shifting Sociologies of the Street." *Sociological Review* 66 (4): 1–15.

Husain, Z., and M. Dutta. 2014. *Women in Kolkata's IT Sector: Satisficing between Work and Household.* New Delhi: Springer.

Jackson, P. 1991. "The Cultural Politics of Masculinity: Towards a Social Geography." *Transactions of the Institute of British Geographers* 16 (2): 199–213.

Jahangir, S., A. Bailey, M. U. Hasan, S. Hossain, M. Helbich, and M. Hyde. 2022. "'When I Need to Travel, I Feel Feverish': Everyday Experiences of Transport Inequalities Among Older Adults in Dhaka, Bangladesh." *Gerontologist* 62 (4): 493–503.

Jeffrey, C. 2010. "Timepass: Youth, Class, and Time among Unemployed Young Men in India." *American Ethnologist* 37 (3): 468–481.

Jeffrey, C., P. Jeffery, and R. Jeffery, eds. 2008. *Degrees without Freedom? Education, Masculinities, and Unemployment in North India.* Stanford, CA: Stanford University Press.

Jha, M. K., and Pushpendra, eds. 2014. *Traversing Bihar: The Politics of Development and Social Justice*. New Delhi: Orient Blackswan.

Joshi, Saakshi, Ajay Bailey, and Anindita Datta, 2021. "On the Move? Exploring Constraints to Accessing Urban Mobility Infrastructures." *Transport Policy* 102: 61–74.

Kandiyoti, D. 1988. "Bargaining with Patriarchy." *Gender and Society* 2: 274–289.

Kantor, H. S. 2020. "Locating the Farmer: Ideologies of Agricultural Labor in Bihar, India." *Anthropology of Work Review* 41 (2): 97–107.

Kenway, J., and A. Hickey-Moody. 2009. "Spatialized Leisure-Pleasures: Global Flows and Masculine Distinctions." *Social & Cultural Geography* 10 (8): 837–852.

Kimmel, M., and M. Mahler. 2003. "Adolescent Masculinity, Homophobia, and Violence: Random School Shootings, 1982–2001." *American Behavioral Scientist* 46 (10): 1439–1458.

Krishnan, S. 2022. "Scooty Girls Are Safe Girls: Risk, Respectability and Brand Assemblages in Urban India." *Social & Cultural Geography* 23 (3): 424–442.

Kumar, A. 2009. "A Class Analysis of the 'Bihari Menace.'" *Economic and Political Weekly* 44 (28): 124–127.

Lamont, M. 2000. *The Dignity of Working Men: Morality and Boundaries of Race, Class, and Immigration*. Cambridge, MA: Harvard University Press.

Larkin, B. 2013. "The Politics and Poetics of Infrastructure." *Annual Review of Anthropology* 42: 327–343.

Lee, D. 2015. "Absolute Traffic: Infrastructural Aptitude in Urban Indonesia." *International Journal of Urban and Regional Research* 39: 234–250.

Little, J. 2002. "Rural Geography: Rural Gender Identity and the Performance of Masculinity and Femininity in the Countryside." *Progress in Human Geography* 26 (5): 665–670.

Longhurst, R. 2000. "Geography and Gender: Masculinities, Male Identity and Men." *Progress in Human Geography* 24 (3): 439–444.

Lumsden, K. 2009. "'Do We Look Like Boy Racers?' The Role of the Folk Devil in Contemporary Moral Panics." *Sociological Research Online* 14 (1). https://doi.org/10.5153/sro.1840.

———. 2013. "Policing the Roads: Traffic Cops, Boy Racers, and Anti-social Behaviour." *Policing and Society* 23 (2): 204–221.

Madan, T. N. 2003. "The Householder Tradition in Hindu Society." In *The Blackwell Companion to Hinduism*, edited by G. Flood, 288–305. Oxford: Blackwell.

Mani, A., M. Pai, and R. Aggarwal. 2012. *Sustainable Urban Transport in India: Role of the Auto-rickshaw Sector.* Bangalore: EMBARQ India.

Marion, R., and A. Eldridge. 2009. *Planning the Night-Time City.* New York: Routledge.

Massey, D. 2005. *For Space.* London: Sage.

Mattingly, C. 1998. *Healing Dramas and Clinical Plots: The Narrative Structure of Experience.* Cambridge: Cambridge University Press.

Mattingly, C., and L. C. Garro, eds. 2000. *Narrative and the Cultural Construction of Illness and Healing.* Berkeley: University of California Press.

Mazumdar, R. 2001. "The Figure of the Bombay Tapori: Language, Gesture and the Cinematic City." *Economic and Political Weekly* 36 (52): 4872–4880.

McDowell, L. 1997. *Capital Culture: Gender at Work in the City.* Oxford: Blackwell.

———. 1999. *Gender, Identity and Place: Understanding Feminist Geographies.* Oxford: Blackwell.

———. 2003. "Masculine Identities and Low-Paid Work: Young Men in Urban Labour Markets." *International Journal of Urban and Regional Research* 27 (4): 828–848.

McFarlane, C., and J. Rutherford. 2008. "Political Infrastructures: Governing and Experiencing the Fabric of the City." *International Journal of Urban and Regional Research* 32(2): 363–374.

McFarlane, C., J. Silver, and Y. Truelove. 2017. "Cities within Cities: Intra-urban Comparison of Infrastructure in Mumbai, Delhi and Cape Town." *Urban Geography* 38 (9): 1393–1417.

McLean, F. 2009. "SUV Advertising: Constructing Identities and Practices." In *Car Troubles: Critical Studies of Automobility*, edited by J. Conley and A. T. McLaren, 59–76. London: Ashgate.

Melbin, M. 1978. "Night as Frontier." *American Sociological Review* 43 (1): 3–22.

Mellström, U. 2004. "Machines and Masculine Subjectivity: Technology as an Integral Part of Men's Life Experiences." *Men and Masculinities* 6 (4): 368–383.

Merry, S. E. 1983. "Urban Danger: Life in a Neighborhood of Strangers." In *Urban Life: Readings in Urban Anthropology*, edited by G. Gmelch and W. P. Zenner, 63–72. Prospect Heights, IL: Waveland Press.

Messerschmidt, J. W. 1993. *Masculinities and Crime: Critique and Reconceptualization of Theory*. Lanham, MD: Rowman & Littlefield.

Mitra, I. 2016. "Recycling the Urban: Migration Settlement in the Question of Labour in Contemporary Kolkata." *Economic and Political Weekly* (26, 27): 55–62.

Mohan, D. 2013. "Moving around in Indian Cities." *Economic and Political Weekly* 48 (30): 40–48.

Mohan, D., and D. Roy. 2003. "Operating on Three Wheels: Auto-Rickshaw Drivers of Delhi." *Economic and Political Weekly* 38: 177–180.

Mohan, D., O. Tsimhoni, M. Sivak, and M. J. Flannagan. 2009. "Road Safety in India: Challenges and Opportunities." UMTRI-2009-1. Ann Arbor: University of Michigan, Transportation Research Institute.

Moi, T. 2019. "Rethinking Character." In *Character: Three Inquiries in Literary Studies*, edited by A. Anderson, R. Felski, and T. Moi, 27–75. Chicago: University of Chicago Press.

Möllering, G. (2001), "The Nature of Trust: From Georg Simmel to a Theory of Expectation, Interpretation and Suspension." *Sociology* 35(2), 403–420.

Mukherjee, S. 2009. "The Biharis of Calcutta." In *Calcutta Mosaic: Essays and Interviews on the Minority Communities of Calcutta*, edited by N. Gupta, H. Banerjee, and S. Mukherjee, 152–163. New Delhi: Anthem Press.

Myers, K. A., K. B. Forest, and S. L. Miller. 2004. "Officer Friendly and the Tough Cop: Gays and Lesbians Navigate Homophobia and Policing." *Journal of Homosexuality* 47 (1): 17–37.

Nair, J. 2014. "Calcutta and Its Anti-economic Economy." In *Strangely Beloved: Writings on Calcutta*, edited by N. Gupta, 53–65. New Delhi: Rupa.

Neve, G. de. 2008. "'We Are All Sondukarar (Relatives)!': Kinship and Its Morality in an Urban Industry of Tamilnadu, South India." *Modern Asian Studies* 42 (1): 211–246.

Newburn, T., and E. Stanko, eds. 1994. *Just Boys Doing Business? Men, Masculinities and Crime.* New York: Routledge.

Nicholls, W. J., and J. Uitermark. 2016. *Cities and Social Movements: Immigrant Rights Activism in the United States, France, and the Netherlands, 1970–2015.* Chichester: Wiley-Blackwell.

Nielsen, K. B. 2010. "Contesting India's Development? Industrialisation, Land Acquisition and Protest in West Bengal." *Forum for Development Studies* 37 (2): 145–170.

Nielsen, K. B., and H. L. Wilhite. 2017. "The Rise and Fall of the 'People's Car': Middle-Class Aspirations, Status and Mobile Symbolism in 'New India.'" In *Cars, Automobility and Development in Asia: Wheels of Change,* edited by A. Hansen and K. B. Nielsen, 171–190. London: Routledge.

Osella, F., and C. Osella. 1999. "From Transience to Immanence: Consumption, Life-Cycle and Social Mobility in Kerala, South India." *Modern Asian Studies* 33 (4): 989–1020.

Oswin, N. 2008. Critical Geographies and the Uses of Sexuality. *Progress in Human Geography* 32 (1): 89–103.

Pain, R. 2000. "Place, Social Relations and the Fear of Crime: A Review." *Progress in Human Geography* 24 (3): 365–388.

Pal, M., and P. Buzzanell. 2008. "The Indian Call Center Experience: A Case Study in Changing Discourses of Identity, Identification, and Career in a Global Context." *Journal of Business Communication* 45 (1): 31–60.

Pandian, Anand. 2008. "Devoted to Development: Moral Progress, Ethical Work, and Divine Favor in South India." *Anthropological Theory* 8 (2): 159–179.

Parichiti and Jagori. 2012. "Women's Safety Audit: A Report on the Safety Audits Conducted in Dhakuria, Bagha Jatin and Ballygunge Stations, Kolkata." http://www.jagori.org/sites/default/files/publication/Parichiti-Jagori-Womens-Safety-Audit-Dec2012.pdf

Parker, B. 2011. "Material Matters: Gender and the City." *Geography Compass* 5(6): 433–447.

———. 2017. *Masculinities and Markets: Raced and Gendered Urban Politics in Milwaukee.* Athens: University of Georgia Press.

Parry, J. 2014. "Sex, Bricks and Mortar: Constructing Class in a Central Indian Steel Town." *Modern Asian Studies* 48 (5): 1242–1275.

Paul, S. 2015. "Informal Labour, Informal Politics: A Case Study of Auto-rickshaw Operators in Kolkata." *SWS-RLS Occasional Paper* 10, School of Women's Studies, Jadavpur University.

Paul, T. 2011. "Space, Gender and Fear of Crime: Some Explorations from Kolkata." *Gender, Technology and Development* 13 (3): 411–435.

———. 2013. "Interrogating the Global/Local Interface: Workplace Interactions in the New Economic Spaces of Kolkata." *Gender, Technology and Development* 17 (3): 337–359.

Peake, L. 2016. "On the Twenty-First Century Quest for Feminism and the Global Urban." *International Journal of Urban and Regional Research* 40 (1): 219–227.

Pease, B. 2009. "Immigrant Men and Domestic Life: Renegotiating the Patriarchal Bargain?" In *Migrant Men: Critical Studies of Masculinities and the Migration Experience*, edited by M. Donaldson, R. Hibbins, R. Howson, and B. Pease, 79–95. London: Routledge.

Pessar, P. R. 1999. "Engendering Migration Studies: The Case of New Immigrants in the United States." *American Behavioral Scientist* 42 (4): 577–600.

Peters, R. 2020. "Motorbike-Taxi-Drivers as Infrastructure in the Indonesian City." *Ethnos* 85 (3): 471–490.

Phadke, S. 2005. "You Can Be Lonely in a Crowd: The Production of Safety in Mumbai." *Indian Journal of Gender Studies* 12 (1): 41–62.

———. 2007. "Dangerous Liaisons: Women and Men; Risk and Reputation in Mumbai." *Economic and Political Weekly* 42 (17): 1510–1518.

———. 2012. "The Gendered Usage of Public Space." In *The Fear That Stalks: Gender-Based Violence in Public Spaces*, edited by S. Pilot and L. Prabhu, 51–80. New Delhi: UNDP and Zubaan.

———. 2013. "Unfriendly Bodies, Hostile Cities: Reflections on Loitering and Gendered Public Space." *Economic and Political Weekly* 48 (39): 50–59.

Phadke, S., S. Khan, and S. Ranade. 2009. "Why Loiter? Radical Possibilities for Gendered Dissent." In *Dissent and Cultural Resistance in Asia's Cities*, edited by M. Butcher and S. Velayutham, 185–203. London: Routledge.

Philip, S. 2022. *Becoming Young Men in a New India: Masculinities, Gender Relations and Violence in the Postcolony.* New Delhi: Cambridge University Press.

Pilot, S., and L. Prabhu, eds. 2012. *The Fear That Stalks: Gender-based Violence in Public Spaces.* New Delhi: UNDP and Zubaan.

Poynting, S., P. Tabar, and G. Noble. 2009. "Looking for Respect." In *Migrant Men: Critical Studies of Masculinities and the Migration Experience,* edited by M. Donaldson, R. Hibbins, R. Howson, and B. Pease, 135–153. New York: Routledge.

Priyadarshini, A. 2014. "The Rhetoric of Development in Contemporary Bihar." In *Traversing Bihar: The Politics of Development and Social Justice,* edited by M. K. Jha and Pushpendra, 63–76. New Delhi: Orient Blackswan.

Probyn, E. 2003. "The Spatial Imperative of Subjectivity." In *Handbook of Cultural Geography,* edited by K. Anderson, M. Domosh, S. Pile, and N. Thrift, 290–299. London: Sage.

Pucher, J., N. Korattyswaropam, N. Mittal, and N. Ittiyerah. 2005. "Urban Transport Crisis in India." *Transport Policy* 12: 185–198.

Ranade, S. 2007. "The Way She Moves: Mapping the Everyday Production of Gender-Space." *Economic and Political Weekly* 42 (17): 1519–1526.

Ray, M. 2012. "This London Dream Has Parts Missing." *The Hindu.* https://www.thehindu.com/opinion/lead/this-london-dream-has-parts-missing/article2904488.ece.

Ray, R. 2000. "Masculinity, Femininity and Servitude: Domestic Workers in Calcutta in the Late Twentieth Century." *Feminist Studies* 26 (3): 691–718.

Ray, R., and S. Qayum. 2009. *Cultures of Servitude: Modernity, Domesticity, and Class in India.* Stanford, CA: Stanford University Press.

Reeves, J. 2006. "Recklessness, Rescue and Responsibility: Young Men Tell Their Stories of the Transition to Fatherhood." *Practice* 18 (2): 79–90.

Roberts, M., and A. Eldridge. 2012. *Planning the Night-Time City.* New York: Routledge.

Roberts, S. 2013. "Boys Will Be Boys . . . Won't They? Change and Continuities in Social Class and Contemporary Young Working-Class Masculinities." *Sociology* 47 (4): 671–686.

Robinson, J. 2006. *Ordinary Cities: Between Modernity and Development.* London: Routledge.

Rodgers, D., and B. O'Neill. 2012. "Infrastructural Violence: Introduction." *Ethnography* 13 (4): 401–412.

Roy, A. 2003. *City Requiem, Calcutta: Gender and the Politics of Poverty.* Minneapolis: University of Minnesota Press.

———. 2004. "The Gentleman's City: Urban Informality in the Calcutta of New Communism." In *Urban Informality: Transnational Perspectives from the Middle East, Latin America, and South Asia,* edited by A. Roy and N. Al Sayyad, 147–170. Lanham, MD: Lexington Books.

———. 2009. "The 21st Century Metropolis: New Geographies of Theory." *Regional Studies* 43 (6): 819–830.

———. 2011. "Slumdog Cities: Rethinking Subaltern Urbanism." *International Journal of Urban and Regional Research* 35: 223–238.

Roy, A., and A. Ong, eds. 2011. *Worlding Cities: Asian Experiments and the Art of Being Global.* Malden, MA: Wiley-Blackwell.

Roy, A. K. 2011. *Distress Migration and Left Behind Women: A Study of Rural Bihar Rawat.* Jaipur: Publications.

Roy, T. 1990. "The Calcutta Metro." In *Calcutta: The Living City,* vol. 2: *The Present and Future,* edited by S. Chaudhuri, 157–160. Calcutta: Oxford University Press.

Sadana, Rashmi. 2010. "On the Delhi Metro: An Ethnographic View," *Economic and Political Weekly* 45(46), November 13–19, 77–83.

Samanta, G., and S. Roy. 2013. "Towards a Subaltern Paradigm of Mobility: Hand-Pulled Rickshaws in Kolkata." *Transfers* 3: 62–68.

Sassen, S. 2000. "New Frontiers Facing Urban Sociology at the Millennium." *British Journal of Sociology* 5 (1): 143–159.

Sayer, A. 2020. "Critiquing—and Rescuing—Character." *Sociology* 54 (3): 460–481.

Schilke, O., M. Reimann, and K. S. Cook. 2021. "Trust in Social Relations." *Annual Review of Sociology* 47: 239–259.

Schiller, N. G., and A. Çağlar. 2009. "Towards a Comparative Theory of Locality in Migration Studies: Migrant Incorporation and City Scale." *Journal of Ethnic and Migration Studies* 35 (2): 177–202.

Schmid, C., O. Karaman, N. C. Hanakata, et al. 2018. "Towards a New Vocabulary of Urbanisation Processes: A Comparative Approach." *Urban Studies* 55 (1): 19–52.

Schrock, D., and M. Schwalbe. 2009. "Men, Masculinity, and Manhood Acts." *Annual Review of Sociology* 35: 277–295.

Scraton, S., and B. Watson. 1998. "Gendered Cities: Women and Public Leisure Space in the Postmodern City." *Leisure Studies* 17 (2): 123–137.

Sedgwick, E. K. 1995. *Between Men: English Literature and Male Homosocial Desire.* New York: Columbia University Press.

Seidler, V. 2006. *Transforming Masculinities: Men, Cultures, Bodies, Power, Sex and Love.* London: Routledge.

Sen, A. 2008. "Violence, Identity and Poverty." *Journal of Peace Research* 45 (1): 5–15.

Sen, Samita. 2016. "Organised Informality: Autorickshaw Drivers in Kolkata." SWS-RLS Occasional Paper 13, School of Women's Studies, Jadavpur University.

Sen, Samita, and N. Sanyal. 2015. *Domestic Days: Women, Work, and Politics in Contemporary Kolkata.* New Delhi: Oxford University Press.

Sen, Siddhartha. 2017. *Colonizing, Decolonizing, and Globalizing Kolkata: From a Colonial to a Post-Marxist City.* Amsterdam: Amsterdam University Press.

Sennett, R. 1998. *Corrosion of Character.* New York: Norton.

———. 2012. *Together: The Rituals, Pleasures and Politics of Co-operation.* London: Penguin.

Shah, A. 2006. "The Labour of Love: Seasonal Migration from Jharkhand to the Brick-Kilns in Other States of India." *Contributions to Indian Sociology* 40 (1): 91–116.

Shah, S. 2014. *Street Corner Secrets: Sex, Work, and Migration in the City of Mumbai.* Raleigh, NC: Duke University Press,

Shahidian, H. 1999. "Gender and Sexuality among Immigrant Iranians in Canada." *Sexualities* 2 (2): 189–222.

Shakthi, S. 2022. "Beyond Respectability? Office Taxis and Gendered Automobility in Urban India." *Mobilities.* https://doi.org/10.1080/17450101.2022.2054355.

Sharma, A., and A. Gupta, eds. 2006. *The Anthropology of the State: A Reader.* Oxford: Blackwell.

Shaw, A. 2012. *Indian Cities: Oxford India Short Introductions.* New Delhi: Oxford University Press.

———. 2015. "Inner-City and Outer-City Neighbourhoods in Kolkata: Their Changing Dynamics Post Liberalisation." *Environment and Urbanization Asia* 6 (2): 139–153.

Sibley, D. 1988. "Purification of Space." *Environment and Planning D: Society and Space* 6: 409–421.

Sikweyiya, Y., R. Jewkes, and R. Morrell. 2007. "Talking about Rape: South African Men's Responses to Questions about Rape." *Agenda* 21 (74): 48–57.

Silvestri, M. 2017. "Police Culture and Gender: Revisiting the 'Cult of Masculinity.'" *Policing: A Journal of Policy and Practice* 11 (3): 289–300.

Simmel, G. 1949. "The Sociology of Sociability." *American Journal of Sociology* 55 (3): 254–261.

———. 1988. "The Metropolis and Mental Life." In *Simmel on Culture,* edited by D. Frisby and M. Featherstone, 174–186. London: Sage.

———. 1990. *The Philosophy of Money.* London: Routledge.

Simone, A. 2004. "People as Infrastructure: Intersecting fragments in Johannesburg." *Public Culture* 16 (3): 407–429.

———. 2008. "Some Reflections on Making Popular Culture in Urban Africa," *African Studies Review* 51 (3): 75–89.

———. 2010. *City Life from Jakarta to Dakar: Movements at the Crossroads.* New York: Routledge.

———. 2014. "Relational Infrastructures in Postcolonial Urban Worlds." In *Infrastructural Lives: Urban Infrastructure in Context,* edited by S. Graham and C. McFarlane, 17–38. London: Routledge.

———. 2016. "City of Potentiality: An Introduction." *Theory, Culture & Society* 33: 5–29.

———. 2019. *Improvised Lives.* Cambridge: Polity.

Singh, Y. P. 2002. "Performance of the Kolkata (Calcutta) Metro Railway: A Case Study." In *Urban Mobility for All,* edited by X. Godard and I. Fatonzoun, 337–342. Tokyo: Balkema.

Sinha, M. 1995. *Colonial Masculinity: The "Manly Englishman" and the "Effeminate Bengali" in the Late Nineteenth Century.* Manchester, UK: Manchester University Press.

———. 1999. "Giving Masculinity a History: Some Contributions from the Historiography of Colonial India." *Gender & History* 11 (3): 445–460.

Sommers, J. 1998. "Men at the Margin: Masculinity and Space in Downtown Vancouver, 1950–1986." *Urban Geography* 19 (4): 287–310.

Sopranzetti, C. 2014. "Owners of the Map: Mobility and Mobilization among Motorcycle Taxi Drivers in Bangkok." *City & Society* 26 (1): 120–143.

Srivastava, S. 1998. *Constructing Post-colonial India: National Character and the Doon School*. London: Routledge.

———. 2001. "Non-Gandhian Sexuality, Commodity Cultures, and a 'Happy Married Life': The Cultures of Masculinity and Heterosexuality in India." *South Asia: Journal of South Asian Studies* 24 (1): 225–249.

———. 2004. "The Masculinity of Dis-Location: Commodities, the Metropolis, and the Sex-Clinics of Delhi and Mumbai," in *South Asian Masculinities: Change and Continuity*, edited by R. Chopra, C. Osella, and F. Osella, 175–223. New Delhi: Women Unlimited.

———. 2010. "Fragmentary Pleasures: Masculinity, Urban Spaces and Commodity Politics in Delhi." *Journal of Royal Anthropological Institute* 16 (4): 835–852.

———. 2012. "Masculinity and Its Role in Gender-Based Violence in Public Spaces." In *The Fear That Stalks: Gender-Based Violence in Public Spaces*, edited by S. Pilot and L. Prabhu, 13–50. New Delhi: UNDP and Zubaan.

———. 2013. "Street, Footpath, Gated Community: On the Cultures of Indian Pornography." In *Sexuality Studies*, edited by S. Srivastava, 228–253. New Delhi: Oxford University Press.

———. 2015. *Entangled Urbanism: Slum, Gated Community, and Shopping Mall in Delhi and Gurgaon*. New Delhi: Oxford University Press.

Stanko, E. 1994. "Challenging the Problem of Men's Individual Violence." In *Just Boys Doing Business? Men, Masculinities and Crime*, edited by T. Newburn and E. Stanko, 32–45. New York: Routledge.

Stuart, F. 2016. "Becoming 'Copwise': Policing, Culture, and the Collateral Consequences of Street-Level Criminalization." *Law and Society Review* 50 (2): 279–313.

Sztompka, P. 1999. *Trust: A Sociological Theory*. Cambridge: Cambridge University Press.

Tetzlaff, S. 2017. "Revolution or Evolution? The Making of the Automobile Sector as a Key Industry in Mid-20th Century India." In *Cars, Automobility and Development in Asia: Wheels of Change*, edited by A. Hansen and K. B. Nielsen, 62–80. London: Routledge.

Thompson, E. C. 2003. "Malay Male Migrants: Negotiating Contested Identities in Malaysia." *American Ethnologist* 30 (3): 418–438.

Tiwari, G. 2007. "Urban Transportation Planning." Seminar 579, Transport for Liveable Cities: A Symposium on the Problems of Urban Transport. https://www.india-seminar.com/2007/579/579_geetam_tiwari.htm.

Tomsen, S., ed. 2008. *Crime, Criminal Justice and Masculinities*. Aldershot: Ashgate.

Tonkiss, F. 2005. *Space, the City and Social Theory*. Cambridge: Polity.

Tripathy, R. 2007. "Bhojpuri Cinema: Regional Resonances in the Hindi Heartland." *South Asian Popular Culture* 5 (2): 145–165.

———. 2013. "Mapping the Invisible World of Bhojpuri Cinema and Its Changing Audience." In *Routledge Handbook of Indian Cinemas*, edited by K. M. Gokulsing, W. Dissanayake, and R. K. Dasgupta, 150–161. London: Routledge.

Uberoi, P. 2006. *Freedom and Destiny: Gender, Family, and Popular Culture in India*. Delhi: Oxford University Press.

Valeur, H. 2014. *India, the Urban Transition: A Case Study of Development Urbanism*. Copenhagen: Architectural Publisher.

Verma, A. 1999. "Cultural Roots of Police Corruption in India." *Policing* 22 (3): 264–228.

Viswanath, K., and S. Mehrotra. 2007. "Shall We Go Out? Women's Safety in Public Spaces in Delhi." *Economic and Political Weekly* 42 (17): 1542–1548.

Vuchic, V. R. 1999. *Transportation for Livable Cities*. New Brunswick, NJ: Rutgers University, Center for Urban Policy Research.

Walker, C., and S. Roberts, eds. 2018. *Masculinity, Labour, and Neoliberalism: Working-Class Men in International Perspective*. New York: Palgrave Macmillan.

Walker, L., D. Butland, and R. W. Connell. 2000. "Boys on the Road: Masculinities, Car Culture, and Road Safety Education." *Journal of Men's Studies* 8 (2): 153–169.

Weiner, M. 1978. *Sons of the Soil: Migration and Ethnic Conflict in India.* Princeton, NJ: Princeton University Press.

Whitehead, A. 2005. "Man to Man Violence: How Masculinity May Work as a Dynamic Risk Factor." *Howard Journal of Criminal Justice* 44 (4): 411–422.

Willis, K., and B. Yeoh, eds. 2000. *Gender and Migration.* Cheltenham: Edward Elgar.

Wilson, E. 1991. *The Sphinx in the City: Urban Life, the Control of Disorder, and Women.* Berkeley: University of California Press.

Wood, P., and A. Latham. 2015. "Inhabiting Infrastructure: Exploring the Interactional Spaces of Urban Cycling." *Environment and Planning A* 47 (2): 300–319.

Yago, G. 1983. "The Sociology of Transportation." *Annual Review of Sociology* 9: 173–190.

Yazici, B. 2013. "Towards an Anthropology of Traffic: A Ride through Class Hierarchies on Istanbul's Roadways." *Ethnos Journal of Anthropology*, 78: 515–542.

Zeiderman, A., S. Ahmad Kaker, J. Silver, and A. Wood. 2015. "Uncertainty and Urban Life." *Public Culture* 27 (2): 281–304.

Filmography

Calcutta Taxi. Directed by Vikram Dasgupta, 2012.

Chippa. Directed by Safdar Rahman, 2019.

Dahan [Crossfire]. Directed by Rituparno Ghosh, 1997.

Dosar [The companion]. Directed by Rituparno Ghosh, 2006.

Mahanagar [The big city]. Directed by Satyajit Ray, 1963.

Meghe Dhaka Tara [The cloud-capped star]. Directed by Ritwik Ghatak, 1960.

Index

About the Author

ROMIT CHOWDHURY is senior lecturer in sociology at Erasmus University College, Rotterdam, the Netherlands. He is an urban sociologist with interests in masculinities, public transport, and everyday life in cities. He is coeditor of *Men and Feminism in India*.